Coffee on the Terrace

Coffee on the Terrace

By
Bruce Grayden

Wycliffe
Partners in Bible Translation
Orlando, Florida
1-800-WYCLIFFE • www.wycliffe.org

Visit Wycliffe's Web site at www.wycliffe.org

Coffee on the Terrace
© 2002 Wycliffe Bible Translators Australia, Inc.
70 Graham Road
Kangaroo Ground VIC 3097
Australia

Revised and reprinted with permission by:
Wycliffe Bible Translators, Inc.
P.O. Box 628200
Orlando, Florida 32862-8200

ISBN 0-938978-30-6

Printed in the United States of America

Table of Contents

Chapter   **Page**

1 Getting There   1

2 Life, Death and Other Mysteries   23

3 Fun Times and Difficult Times   47

4 Another World   59

5 In the Thick of Things   77

6 Quitting Time   103

7 Worth Waiting For   119

8 New Experiences   131

9 Nervous Times   153

10 The Importance of Drinking Coffee   171

11 Cause for Rejoicing   195

    Epilogue   205

    Afterword   207

ONE

Getting There

Why Bible Translation and the Philippines?

I t was delicious coffee, and although I'd already had more than what I considered "safe" to drink before my heart started palpitating, I couldn't and didn't resist the latest offer. Beautifully lost in the last mouthful of the thick, sweet, pre-lunch coffee offered to Kilaw, Palongpong and me, I was suddenly brought back to earth by a woman's scream. All heads turned towards the open doorway. Women and children, most of them crying loudly, were running past the house, their mouths wide open in terror.

Kilaw rushed outside. I had no wish to follow. The only time I had seen people so terrified was when someone was controlled by a spirit, and since I had discovered rather uncomfortably a couple of years earlier that dealing with spirits was not one of my gifts, I was quite happy to stay right where I was.

I heard Kilaw calling, "If that's what you want, bring him out and kill him here in front of everyone, but you'll have to kill me too!" What did he mean? I hadn't heard anyone talk to the spirits like that before.

He came back to the house three times for whispered conversations with Palongpong. They both seemed anxious about whatever was going on, but I didn't move from where I was safely ensconced. After the third time, however, by now rather curious, I asked Palongpong, "What's going on?"

He looked at me for several seconds then spoke softly, his voice shaky. "There are two men with guns, and they want to shoot someone!"

1

Getting There

"Who?"
"You!"
"Me!"
Shoot me? This wasn't why we had come to the Philippines!

Why Bible translation and the Philippines?

Judith and I became Christians as teenagers. From
very early in our Christian life, we both had a desire to
tell the good news about Jesus to people who had never heard
of Him. During the next four years we went to the regular
meetings of three mission agencies and heard lots of missionaries speak at our church. Those who grabbed our attention
the most talked about Bible translation.

Then in 1967 at a Christian Endeavour camp in Victoria,
we heard David Cummings, Australian Director of Wycliffe,
speak. He used 1 Corinthians 14:8 as his text: "If the bugler
doesn't sound a clear call, how will the soldiers know they are
being called to battle?" (NLT)

"Suppose soldiers are waiting to go into battle," he said,
"and the bugler is told to play Advance. If the sound that
comes out of the bugle is not clear, the soldiers won't know
what their leader is saying because the sound is uncertain. It's
a lot like that when people hear the Word of God in a language
they don't understand. They hear sound, but they don't know
what God is saying to them."

He had our attention. We began to think about the implications for us. We loved to read the Word of God, the Bible, and
took for granted that it was in English. If it were only available
in a language we didn't know, how would we understand it?
How big a problem was this to the millions who don't have
access to the Bible in a language they can understand? If we
were to help translate it for a group of people who didn't have
it in their own language, that would give them the opportunity
to know what God wanted to say to them personally, too. We
both knew what God wanted us to do.

2

In 1968 Judith and I were married, and in 1969 we went to
the Bible College of Victoria. After three good years of studying the Bible, during which time our first two children, David
and Elizabeth, were born, we attended the Summer Institute of
Linguistics (SIL) to learn how to analyse unwritten languages
and to translate.

During our Bible College years we had often prayed, "Lord,
where do you want us to serve you?" We thought, We'll probably go to Papua New Guinea. Isn't that where all Australians
go? But it didn't feel right. Then we met Rosemary Rodda, a
translator working in the Philippines. Ro was a tutor at our
first SIL course, and on our second day there we asked her,
"Would you tell us about the Philippines?"

Ro smiled broadly, took a deep breath, and began to talk.
During the next ten weeks she told us about the Philippines,
its people, and the great need for translators, and by the end
of the course we were convinced not only about the country
where God wanted us to go but even the language group—
the Bangingi in the southern Philippines.

We applied to Wycliffe Bible Translators and were accepted
as members in March 1972 and assigned to work in the
Philippines. Sixteen months later, after attending the Pacific
Orientation Course in Papua New Guinea, then a more
advanced linguistic course, and finally building up a team
of what would prove to be very faithful prayer and financial
supporters, we left for Manila, eager to begin our work
amongst the Bangingi.

On our arrival, however, we were disappointed to hear that
all new members were required to study Tagalog, the national
language, before doing anything else. But it would take nine
months! What about the Bangingi? We wanted to start work
amongst them.

As far as we were concerned, the main redeeming features
were that those nine months would give us a good introduction to Philippine culture and climate and also the

Getting There

opportunity to learn in a classroom setting what made Philippine languages "tick."

Therefore, instead of catching a boat to the southern Philippines, we caught a bus to Lipa City, 80 km south of Manila, found a house to rent, and prepared to make the most of the "delay." The delay was extended even further when we found that classes wouldn't begin for another month. We decided to visit some translators in the mountains north of Manila to get an idea of what was ahead of us.

Our first stop was Amganad, a village nestled amongst the famous rice terraces of Banaue, said to be 3,000 years old and known locally as "The Eighth Wonder of the World." An American colleague, Anne West, had been working there for several years.

As we wandered around the village, we were startled by the sight of a human skull. Anne pointed to cloth bundles under most of the houses. Amganad people venerate their ancestors and keep their bones as a mark of respect. Each year the bones are unwrapped, washed, carefully rewrapped, and returned to their special places under the houses again. It all felt just a little eerie to us, though obviously not to the village people.

It was good hearing about the church that had been started in Amganad and about the new believers enjoying their recently translated Scriptures.

Gazing in wonder at countless rice terraces etched into the towering mountains so that they looked like giant staircases carpeted in emerald green, we couldn't help thinking, "What a magnificent place to live!"

But not, of course, for us. Nothing was going to sidetrack us...not even the promise of cool, fresh, relaxed mountain evenings, the friendliness and hospitality of the people...and the many other attractions of the region. We were heading south to a tropical island, with the promise of oppressive heat by day and little, if any, respite at night.

Those mountains, however, certainly looked attractive.

4

The next day we flew to Balangao, ten minutes north of Amganad by small plane, to visit Joanne Shetler, another American translator. Jo had worked there for ten years. After a heart-in-mouth landing on a narrow, sloping strip shorter than an aircraft carrier, and a cautious hike along the tightrope-like edges of rice terraces that serve as paths, we reached Jo's house. Balangao's rice-terraced mountain sides were breathtaking, their beauty surpassing even those around Amganad.

For five too-short hours we chatted with Jo and some of her Balangao friends and listened spellbound to the story of the birth of the Balangao church. Several believers testified to the impact of the translated Scriptures on their lives. The most vocal was Canao, one of the Balangao church elders.

Canao was Jo's village "father." When Jo and her first colleague, Anne Fetzer, had gone to Balangao almost a decade earlier, Canao had been shocked to discover that the American linguists they were expecting to come and live with them were women. He said to the ladies, "Don't you know it's not safe for women to be here? We're headhunters!"

They already knew that! What they hadn't anticipated was the reaction of Canao to their plight. He said, "You need someone to care for you. You don't have your fathers with you to do that, so I will be your father." A beautiful family relationship began right there and then, and after Anne left later to be married, it continued with Jo until Canao's death some 20 years later.

As we stood up to leave, Canao pointed to a nearby mountain range and declared, "I'm going to pray that God will send you to the people over there, the Southern Kalingas."

"We appreciate your interest," we said, "but we're heading for the southern Philippines, about 2,000 kilometres from here. That's where God wants us to go, and nothing is going to sidetrack us!"

Getting There

All is not as it seems?

Returning to Lipa City, we began Tagalog language study and quickly found it useful. Although English is widely spoken as a second language in the Philippines, our Australian dialect was not easily understood. We needed to speak Tagalog if we were going to communicate well.

One time when Judith went into a drug store (pharmacy), which doubled as a grocery store, and asked for Neosporin ointment, the salesgirl looked puzzled for a moment and then brought her a can of Campbell's soup. Another time, when I tried to buy a pot scourer, the salesgirl understood none of my frustrated attempts to make clear what I wanted and kept insisting she had none. The more she insisted, the more frustrated I became trying to make it clear what I wanted. I could see several pot scourers on a rack right behind her. But I had learned it would embarrass her if I pointed them out to her and caused her to realise she had made a mistake. I had to walk out of there empty-handed.

Sometimes our Aussie English wasn't even understood by Americans. Once when another Aussie and I were discussing something quite animatedly, some of our American colleagues were standing nearby, and the more excited we became the more agitated they seemed. Finally, one interrupted us and said, "If I didn't know you were good friends, I'd swear you were having an argument!" Another said, "I know you're speaking English, but I can't understand a word you're saying."

There were other little experiences for us too, which could also come under the heading of "Culture Shock." Once when Tisa, the head of the Filipino kitchen staff at SIL's guest house in Manila, saw me, she said in Tagalog, "You're fat." I was pleased to learn that she was actually giving me a compliment, though! To be "fat" is to be healthy.

We noticed the house numbers in one Manila street went like this: 101, 103, 105, 81, 83, 85, 87, 111.... We never found out why, but we did discover it wasn't unusual.

Tagalog grammar was quite a challenge. The variety of prefixes and suffixes that can be attached to a word, and the different meanings created by each affix, continually bewildered us. I remember struggling one night with some aspect of the grammar that was totally different to anything in English. In complete frustration I closed the book and cried out, "What in the world are we doing here?"

A child's voice came from the next room: "We belong to Jesus. That's why we're here!" It was our son David, aged four. I reopened the book and had another look at the problem. I didn't complain again...at least not for a while.

We picked up some of the language in a more relaxed setting through Lolit, a young lady who helped Judith with the housework and looked after our children while we studied. David and Elizabeth took to her immediately, and a lovely friendship developed. Lolit later gave her life to the Lord, and we were privileged to sponsor her through Bible college. She has since married and has been working in a church for several years. She calls us "Mum" and "Dad." She's a very special "daughter" to us.

As we were leaving for language school one morning, David said, "Bye. We'll pray for you as you go." Then they went to the bedroom window to wave to us. When we got outside on the footpath, we looked up and saw them on their knees praying on the window ledge. Then they waved. They looked beautiful.

One day while on a picnic, David was upset when he let his balloon go and it quickly soared into the sky. At bedtime that night, he said, "It's okay. Jesus has my balloon. He's going to keep it till I go up there. When we go up to heaven, our sins will be left down here. And do you know what we'll find in heaven? A balloon! My balloon!"

Getting There

And Elizabeth prayed, "Jesus, thank you for dying on the cross for us, so we can go to heaven and be with you and our balloon."

The streets of Manila are never silent. Always crowded, with cars weaving impatiently through noisy chaos, at times it seems that the system works only because taxi and bus drivers have either rosary beads or rabbits' feet, or both, hanging from their rear vision mirrors.

Our occasional trips to Manila by bus were always stimulating, for want of a more descriptive word. It seemed to us that to qualify as a bus driver, a man didn't need to be crazy, but it certainly helped. The way they drove told us that the ability to drive was apparently only a minor qualification.

We were fascinated at the way the conductor operated. He walked from the front of the bus to the back four times during the first 20 minutes of the journey. First he ascertained the destination of each of the perhaps 60 passengers. Then, after punching the date, time, departure point and destination point on each of 60 tickets, he handed them one by one to the passengers. Then he collected money from each passenger. Finally he handed out any change required, and all from memory. It also amazed us how, on buses that had only one wall and no centre aisle, the conductor shuffled along the running board on the outside of the bus, totally unconcerned about the danger involved as he did his job at 100 km/h or even faster.

Soon after the start of one bus trip, we noticed the driver make the sign of the cross and we wondered what sort of a wild ride we were in for that day. Then we noticed we were passing the cathedral, and that was just something he did as a Catholic.

Once, after a quick trip to Manila for mail and groceries, I waited beside the road for three hours under the boiling sun for a bus, but none of the many that came along stopped because they were all packed. Finally, one bus, which was also packed, surprisingly began to slow down as it approached me. Volkmar, another language school student, was sitting in the front seat, and he had seen me and asked the driver to stop for me. I waved when I saw Volkmar, relieved and grateful for his obvious intervention. However, instead of stopping, the driver immediately accelerated and sped off without me! I realised too late that the way I waved gave the driver the signal, "No, I don't need a ride, thanks." The extra two hours I had to wait in the sun before finally collapsing on a bus passed very slowly.

I rode towards home that day on an ancient bus that I'm sure hit every one of the countless potholes in the road. Shielding my sweaty forehead from the fierce sun, I watched a terrified mouse dodging dozens of attacking feet as it scurried back and forth under the seats. Amusement turned to amazement as 22 extra passengers were crammed into our already overfilled bus because theirs had broken down. The expressions on the faces of people along the road told me how packed the bus was, but there was not a single murmur from any of the passengers.

Amidst all this, a thought entirely unrelated to my present situation suddenly popped into my mind: "Thank you, Lord, for bringing us to the Philippines."

Tricycles are remarkable, too, as they are motor bikes with covered sidecars. We once saw a pig tied onto the luggage rack of a tricycle. Another time we saw a tricycle straining to negotiate a steep hill, a total of ten people sitting and standing on it, all holding bags of market purchases.

The mail system also fascinated us. A letter sent from Manila by ordinary mail took only one day to reach us in Lipa, but another sent by "special delivery" took six days—we were told there's a lot of paperwork with special delivery items! Letters sent by ordinary mail from Manila to Bagabag, 300 km north of Manila, arrived at least a week earlier than letters sent by airmail. Letters marked "airmail" had to go by airmail—

even though the nearest airport was 200 km further north of Bagabag—in order to fulfill the wishes of the sender. Then they would come back to Bagabag by road.

To Bangingi or not to Bangingi?

One morning, about four months into our Tagalog study, we both woke up feeling uneasy about going to the Bangingi. We tried to push a growing uneasiness from our minds, but it persisted. Why were we feeling that way? God wanted us to go to the Bangingi. That fact was very clear to us long before we arrived in the Philippines.

However, over the next few days any enthusiasm we had about going to the Bangingi rapidly diminished until we didn't want to go there at all.

Confused, we prayed a lot about the situation, but nothing changed. We simply had no peace about going to the Bangingi. We wrote to Chuck Walton, who looked after the translation teams assigned to the southern Philippines, to tell him how we felt. A colleague, Jackie Ruch, was in his office when our letter arrived. She told us later that after Chuck read our letter, he said, "If they don't go to the Bangingi, I think I'll be sick."

Then we heard that two of our colleagues, JoAnn Gault from the U.S. and Eunice Diment from England, who had completed their Tagalog study just before we started, decided they would like to work with the Bangingi. So we said to them, "If you believe that's the Lord's will for you, then please go." They did.

(Eighteen months later, Eunice was kidnapped by rebels and a ransom was demanded for her release. I remember thinking, it could have been me! Many people prayed for Eunice's release, and we were all relieved when she was released unharmed after three weeks in captivity.)

Meanwhile, we asked Dan Weaver, our director in Manila, for an assignment in the northern Philippines. Why north? We didn't know. We just felt drawn in that direction. Dan agreed to consider our request, though not before three attempts to convince us of other urgent needs in the south besides the Bangingi.

A few weeks later, he wrote offering us three choices in the north—Central Benguet, Southern Benguet and Kankanay. The first two were close to Baguio, considered the summer capital of the Philippines. Its altitude—a mile above sea level—brought welcome relief when missionaries wanted a cool break from the oppressive lowland heat. We replied, "Dan, either of those three locations will be fine, although we'd prefer one of the two in Benguet."

Three weeks later, we received the much-awaited letter from Dan. He wrote, "You have been assigned to work with the Kankanay." It was our third choice, but it didn't matter. We were happy. Next day we went to Manila to talk with Dan about our plans.

Waiting for us at the guesthouse was another letter from Dan. It consisted of just two sentences: "Your assignment has been changed. Instead of Kankanay, you are to go to Southern Kalinga."

We were stunned. We had read about the Kalingas—they were headhunters! We knew that getting involved in the culture was important, but how fully would we need to? This part of the culture seemed a definite health hazard! How could we even consider for a moment exposing our children to obvious risk? Not at all happy about our assignment, we opened the front door of the guesthouse to get some air and found Jo Shetler standing outside about to come in. Noticing our distress, she took each of us by an arm and asked what was wrong.

As we began to explain our predicament, Jo interrupted us. "I know some Kalingas," she said calmly. "They're lovely people. In fact, the ancestors of many Balangaos were Kalingas. Let's go to the ice cream parlour and talk about it!"

Getting There

A couple of hours and several scoops of delicious magnolia ice cream later, our heads were much clearer. Jo had convinced us it was okay to go to the Kalinga people group.

Finding a village and a home

Our Tagalog study finally completed, we moved north to the SIL Centre on the outskirts of Bagabag. After our village home, Bagabag was to become a second home for us since we would spend at least three months there every year at translation workshops.

At last we were free to get down to the "real" work...the real reason we had come to the Philippines.

Before beginning, I had to take a trip to the Southern Kalinga area to meet the civil authorities and to determine which of its twelve villages would be the best location for us to live and work. A colleague, Dick Gieser, accompanied me. Earlier, Dick had done a survey of several Kalinga languages, including Southern Kalinga, to determine language boundaries and translation needs. His knowledge of the area would be enormously valuable to us.

As we climbed into the small SIL plane to fly to Guinaang, the village where Dick and Ruth Gieser had lived for many years while translating the Scriptures for a neighbouring Kalinga group, I jokingly said to Dick, "We'd like a village about 3,000 feet above sea level." The air at that altitude would be cooler than in the lowlands, giving us some respite from the normally oppressive heat. He laughed and, no doubt with his tongue securely in his cheek, said, "I'll see what I can do!"

From the air, the edges of thousands of rice terraces winding around steep mountain sides looked like a child's scribble on green coloured paper.

On the way, we flew over three Southern Kalinga villages and the pilot, George Fletcher, circled so I could take photos. I took lots! I felt quite emotional as I looked down at the area in which we would soon be living and working.

Five minutes later, we landed at Guinaang. It was there that I was offered my first taste of Kalinga hospitality, in the form of strong, sweet black coffee. It was delicious. For lunch we had rice and beans. Dinner brought a repeat of the lunch menu.

A group of old men gathered together that afternoon to talk. They knew the Southern Kalinga area, and when Dick told them our plans, they suggested our family should live in Arngikan, a small village of about 80 people between Mallango and Sumachor. They said that Sumachor, with 1,600 inhabitants and no toilets, was too dirty. Mallango, with fewer people, was clean but became very muddy in the rainy season. The people in Bangad, situated on the single road that passed through the region, had a lot of contact with outsiders passing through and had adopted several words from other languages.

Early next morning, full of beans, rice and strong coffee, Dick and I set off on a strenuous six-hour hike through the mountains to Lubuagan, a town on the road.

As I entered Lubuagan, absolutely exhausted, I met my first Southern Kalinga man. He was from Mallango, and he was drunk. Our conversation was brief and unproductive, and he staggered away, leaving me with a mixture of excitement and disappointment.

After a restless night, followed by a three-hour wait under a scorching sun for a bus and a bumpy 20 km ride south, we arrived at Tinglayan, the municipal centre of Southern Kalinga.

The mayor of Tinglayan was happy to hear that "Americanos" (all foreigners are called "Americanos" regardless of their country of origin) wanted to come and live in his municipality and felt that Mallango, situated between the two largest villages, Bangad and Sumachor, would be the ideal place for us. Since I had arrived with a letter of introduction from the Secretary of Education and Culture in Manila, the mayor sent a return letter to the Secretary, expressing his pleasure at being able to welcome us to Southern Kalinga.

Getting There

While he was speaking, George Liban, Principal of the Tinglayan Municipal School, came into the mayor's office. When he heard where we were going, he exclaimed, "What a coincidence. I live at Mallango. I'll be going there tomorrow. You go ahead and when I arrive, I will help you find a house to rent."

Grateful for his offer, and with a slightly more confident spring in my nervous step, we hitched a ride on a passing truck and continued our journey.

At the spot where the trail to Mallango leaves the road, we met the *barrio* captain (the village leader), an old man named Kissub. Curious, he listened quietly as we explained why we were there. I was full of questions and rather keen to learn more about their headhunting stories.

As soon as I mentioned that subject, however, I realised, partly from the puzzled expression on Kissub's face, that it may not have been very wise to do so! Things may have come to a "head" right there and then! However, obviously sensing my apprehension, Kissub tried to put me at ease. He said, "There's no need to be afraid. You'll be quite safe here. No heads have been taken in this area for several months."

The most recent incident had occurred just 200 metres from where I then rather numbly stood staring.

With Kissub's "assurance" regarding my well-being sitting just a little uneasily in my mind, I followed closely behind him along the narrow, uneven trail that snaked around the tops of the rice terrace walls, heading for Mallango village.

I struggled to keep up with Kissub, 35 years my senior. I was to observe later that on a dry day the locals could reach Mallango in 20 minutes. It took me 30. On a wet day they could make it in 30 minutes. It took me 45, and if I couldn't sneak out of the village unobserved, children would follow me and laugh whenever I slipped and fell, which I inevitably did on the muddy trail. I only fell down into a rice terrace once, but that incident remained in the minds of those active observers for many years and was laughingly brought to my attention again and again.

As we walked, Kissub told me, in good English, how Mallango was first settled. In 1921, two brothers and their wives from Sumachor, a large village to the south, decided to live and farm there. Others later joined them, and by 1931 more than 50 people had moved there. All were related to each other. "Today," he went on, "Mallango has 110 houses, crammed together in two very tight rows along the top of a ridge. The steep slopes on either side make it difficult for enemies to attack us."

Entering Mallango, I was invited into Kissub's home to eat. It didn't take Judith and me long to learn how wonderfully hospitable Kalinga people are. Eating is a central part of visiting, and in our early months there we were often served chicken. The people were poor and couldn't afford to kill their meagre livestock, so we were glad when we were eventually considered "normal" members of the village and people stopped treating us so royally.

After I ate, Kissub offered me a mug of black coffee. It was very strong, very sweet, and very welcome. After I drank it, he said, "Now that you have drunk our coffee, we consider you to be as much a part of our village as the rest of us who live here are, and we are prepared to die to protect you just as we would anyone else in our village."

I drank lots of coffee after that! I became such a "good" coffee drinker that someone nicknamed me "Fattiig." The real Fattiig, long dead by then, was a legend throughout the whole area, chiefly as a warrior but also for his coffee-drinking.

There was something about that name, though, that intrigued me—people laughed whenever they called me Fattiig, but no one would tell me why! Perhaps I matched his performance as a coffee drinker but looked anything but the warrior that he was. Whatever the reason for their mirth, I didn't mind, as long as they remembered their promise.

Getting There

There were some people who, whenever they saw me drinking coffee, would call out good-naturedly, "Kapi kan uwam!" Literally the words mean "Coffee is only yours," but it's actually an idiomatic expression which means "Coffee's all you live for!"

After eating what was rapidly becoming my staple diet of rice and beans and talking late into the night with extremely hospitable Mallango people who kept feeding me rice and beans, I was happy to crawl into my sleeping bag, absolutely exhausted.

The combination of an uncomfortable wooden floor, my unfit, weary limbs, and the thrill of actually being in the place where we would translate the Bible added up to a restless night. But I didn't really mind.

After a very early morning wake-up call from a loud choir of roosters, Dick and I spent the day chatting with people and eating—rice and one type of bean for breakfast, rice and another type of bean for lunch, and rice and pumpkin for dinner. I welcomed the variety…and of course, there was plenty of coffee.

I had ample time to observe the surroundings. There was very little grass within the boundary of the village, and the only vegetables I could see growing were chokoes. Around the village perimeter were dozens of tall coffee trees. The surrounding mountains were patterned with rice terraces, vegetable gardens and trees.

The terraced rice paddies rise like steps from the river and look majestic when covered with newly growing rice plants. In the dry season the people depend on irrigation for their fields, and water from a spring wends its way along narrow channels, around and through each terrace from the highest to the lowest field. Men have to guard the water going to their terraces at night so that no one will divert the water from their fields to get more for themselves.

Since most gardens are a long way from the village, the older, frailer people usually make shelters in their gardens so they can stay for several days without having to make the strenuous hike back and forth from the village every day.

Several people talked about the "advantages" of Mallango over other villages. "There are no malarial mosquitoes here," they said, "and few rats and flies, and Mallango is never damaged by typhoons, whereas the other villages have everything." Within a few months of moving in, however, we gave them 1 out of 4 for observation. They were right about the mosquitoes. I had to go to the lowlands to get malaria.

It didn't take me long to notice something unique about this place—men never washed the dishes. I knew I could handle living in Mallango quite well.

There's no electricity in Mallango, nor in any of the other villages in Southern Kalinga. And there are no toilets. The pigs take care of the cleaning up. Since it was cold and wet, carrying a long stick was necessary when I went to relieve myself, not just to help me negotiate the slippery mountain slope to a secluded spot but also to keep hungry pigs at bay.

Some people grew tobacco, and I was intrigued not only by the length of the cigars that they made from it, around 20-25 cm, but particularly by the way the women smoked them—with the lighted end inside their mouths. They lasted longer that way! I had heard of people having "fire in the belly," but I didn't fancy it in my mouth.

Most men had just one shirt, which they wore until it almost fell off their backs. We found later that we could recognise people from a great distance by their shirt colour and were usually only mistaken or confused when they changed their shirts. Few wear the traditional clothes now, preferring Western clothes which are more versatile—

when the g-string (loin cloth) is worn by a man planting rice, he has to tuck it well up to keep it out of the mud.

The whole day passed without any sight of Mr. Liban. But just when I felt I couldn't stay awake any longer that night, someone reported that he had at last arrived and would see us in the morning. At least the day, though tiring, had not been wasted—I had chatted with several folk, learned some things about the place, and had begun learning some words.

We woke with everyone else before 5 a.m., drank what was to become my mandatory before-I-attempt-anything-else two mugs of coffee, and then Kissub took us to see Mr. Liban. As we talked together about suitable accommodation, Mr. Liban said, "My house is really the most suitable." Although small, his was one of the largest houses in the village and had two floors. His family would occupy the ground floor and ours the top. The rent would be 50 pesos a month (about $5).

Kissub suggested that I return with my family two weeks later, on September 4. He would wait for us at the road. I agreed, hoping that would give us enough time to prepare.

Our big move

Back at Bagabag, we began packing for our move to Mallango. With our third child due in only two months, I was constantly amazed at Judith's commitment. Nothing was going to stop us beginning our new adventure. It wasn't hard to keep our cargo to a minimum, because we didn't have many possessions, but there were certain things we felt sure we would need. One item was a water-seal toilet—it would be the only toilet in Mallango.

On September 3, we woke early and by 7 a.m. were on our way in a hired truck, driven by the owner. The road to Bontoc, the last major town before Mallango, was surprisingly dry so we arrived there before noon, about three hours earlier than anticipated. We thought about continuing on to Mallango, only about four hours further on, but decided to wait until the next day since we weren't expected until then.

When our driver realised we wanted to go further, he was visibly shocked. "But that's headhunting country!" he exclaimed. "It's not safe there. I cannot go!"

We thought we had explained our itinerary carefully enough when we had first spoken to him about the trip, but it was now quite obvious that he had misunderstood. He had thought we were only going as far as Bontoc. However, after several minutes of discussion about our predicament if he were to leave us in Bontoc, he nervously agreed to take us the whole way. And while we slept in a local inn that night, he slept in his truck to protect our possessions. We prayed he wouldn't dump them during the night and leave.

Relieved to find both driver and truck still there next morning, we left Bontoc after breakfast and arrived at the trail to Mallango less than three hours later.

Kissub was there waiting, though as it turned out not for us but for a bus to Tabuk, the provincial capital. He had forgotten we were coming that day. However, he arranged with some others to carry our cargo to Mallango.

Our driver, afraid he would run out of petrol on the way back to Bontoc and find himself stranded in headhunting country, left as soon as the truck was unloaded, and we never saw him again. We were assured, however, that he did reach home safely.

By nightfall, all but the water-seal toilet had arrived. It finally arrived, well after dark, accompanied by a great amount of laughter. No one had wanted to be seen carrying it, but someone finally offered to and word about its imminent arrival got around quickly so that the carrier attracted a lot of attention after all.

Entering the house where we would live, we were a little dismayed to discover that instead of half the house, we were

Getting There

allocated only half of the top floor—one small room would be our bedroom, kitchen and storeroom, while an even smaller room would be our dining room and study. Mr. Liban had not been able to buy timber to partition the lower area yet, so his family had not completely vacated the top floor.

After sharing the house for a few months, he told us about a house for sale along the road. The price was P8,000 (about $800 then). Since that house was even bigger than the one we were all living in, and the Libans were interested in it, we agreed to pay our rent ten years in advance to allow them to buy it. They dismantled their new home and the pieces were carried to Mallango where it was rebuilt. And when the Liban family moved into their new home, we had all the space we needed.

During our first few weeks in Mallango, we did little but observe and chat with people. Formal work would wait until we made friends and let the village people see we could be trusted. We knew nothing of their language and culture, of course, but we knew that a good knowledge of both was vital if we were to give them God's Word in a way that they would understand.

Our children were important ingredients in relationship building. Children are very precious in Mallango families, and ours were quickly accepted by adults and children alike, as if they had been born there. The adults treated them as they did their own. And our children felt right at home from the start.

On our second day in the village, David, then five years old, had already begun language learning in his own way. We laughed when we saw what he was doing. Surrounded by a helpful group of people, he was having someone write words down as he gave instructions: "'Mother' in your language. 'Baby' in your language. 'House' in your language...."

Whenever the village kids were outside playing, our kids were right there with them, enjoying the fun even before they

knew much of the language. Children don't always need
language to communicate.

Sometimes David went with his friends Franco and
Ferdinand and others to gather firewood. It took them a whole
morning if they had to go deep into the forest to find it. On
hot days, with heavy loads on their young shoulders, they
would stop at the brook, strip down (to underwear for David,
to bare skin for the others) and swim for half an hour. They
often went hiking to nearby mountains and usually found
things to eat on the way—guavas and bananas from planta-
tions and the occasional cicada, which they roasted.

Another highlight of life in Mallango for David was building and riding *tartallak* (homemade go-carts). Riding and
repairing them consumed much of his playtime. They took
their go-carts to different places to try and increase the thrill
of the ride—down to the granaries behind the school; along a
steep path around a ridge; down the airstrip, the fastest and
most thrilling ride of all for them.

One day they built a huge five-wheeler go-cart. It was so
long that it needed a fifth wheel in the middle to support the
weight and stop it sagging to the ground. It even had a steering
wheel. But it didn't last long. It abruptly broke apart on the
first sharp bend!

Judith was seven months pregnant when we arrived in
Mallango, so that added to the people's interest in us, since
most families there had many children. Most couples had five
or six children. One lady had given birth to 23, but only 6 were
now living, the rest having died before they reached their tenth
birthday.

My days usually started around 5.30 a.m. with a wander
through the village, "hunting for coffee" as people described it.
I repeated the exercise every evening at dusk.

Getting There

Drinking coffee was an excellent way to learn the language. It meant I was out with people, engaged in conversation for regular periods every day, whether I felt like it or not. The delicious coffee was an added bonus.

TWO
Life, Death and Other Mysteries

Introductions to Kalinga life and death

The day before we arrived in Mallango a
four-year-old boy died from bronchial
pneumonia. Although not at all keen to see
a dead child, Judith and I wanted to go and pay
our respects to the family, just like everyone else. Outside the
child's house, dozens of men sat talking and drinking liquor;
inside, women and children were chatting.

We expected to hear crying, but no one seemed very upset.
Few were paying any attention to the child's body, which was
wrapped in a clean blanket with only his face showing. He was
seated upright on a bamboo chair with sheaves of rice at his
feet. We wondered about the significance of the rice sheaves
but decided this was not the time to ask.

Afterwards, when we told David and Elizabeth about the
child, they immediately bolted out the door, ran to the house,
and flopped down on the floor in front of the dead boy. It was
the first time they had seen a dead body, and we hadn't wanted
this particular one, a child around their own age, to be the
first. Surprisingly, it didn't upset them at all. This aspect of
Mallango life and culture quickly became part of our life. In
fact, to Mallango people, death is just a part of life since it
occurs too often.

During our first week in Mallango, we also attended
a wedding feast for Kissub's daughter, Ipin. The whole
village turned out for it. It was our first opportunity to
witness one of the most beautiful aspects of the culture, the

23

dancing. About 20 take part each time, with 10 men in one line and 10 women in another. The men beat brass gongs in a distinct rhythmic pattern as they move around in a semicircle. The women, dancing with hands on hips or with arms spread out like wings, form an inner circle.

Wanting to be involved as much as possible in the local culture, we happily, though nervously, joined in when the invitation came. Several laughed at our awkwardness, but we enjoyed trying, and dozens of onlookers told us they appreciated our efforts.

It was a little hard to completely enjoy the occasion, however, after someone told me that the handle of the gong I was holding was a human jawbone! I really wasn't quite ready to come to grips with that part of the culture yet!

We were intrigued later in the day to see one of the old men, the upper half of his body heavily tattooed, dancing in the middle of the circling men and women. He had taken a head sometime in the past and was therefore considered a warrior. His tattoos announced this loud and clear to everyone, and his status entitled him to dance in this place of honour. Over the next few years, people occasionally joked that I should get tattooed, too, but I wasn't prepared to carry out the prerequisite for it—taking a head! The tattooing method didn't exactly attract me either—it's done using a needle dipped in a mixture of pine and sugarcane juices.

Until recently, women have also traditionally been tattooed on their upper torsos and arms, but purely for beautification purposes. However, the practice is dying out as today's generation of young women don't have the same desire for beauty, since it hurts so much to look beautiful.

During the day, after some men sang about the happy occasion and their thankfulness that we had come to live with them, I was asked to make a speech. As I shared how we came to be there and what we hoped to do, Judith noticed a couple of ladies searching for lice in Elizabeth's hair! They were surprised to find none.

The fact that they felt free to do that with one of our children made us feel we were very welcome.

Learning the language

In 1974, there were over 11,000 Southern Kalinga people. We were anxious to give them God's Word, but before we could begin translation, we needed to learn their language. Not a single word had ever been written down.

We started spending several hours each day, either with individuals or with groups of people, writing down words we heard and trying to guess what they meant in English. Finding the right English equivalent wasn't always easy, particularly with concepts that we couldn't see or touch.

Finding people was never a problem—there were always plenty around, often right inside our house. We used to joke that when people had nothing to do they came to our place to do it. There was never a problem finding people; getting them to help us learn their language was sometimes a problem though.

At special events in the village, like the wedding feast, we had observed how people would sit for many hours without moving. But when we wanted them to teach words to us, and then repeat them over and over until we could pronounce them correctly, few would sit with us for even one hour. Most had a reason for their sudden departure—usually something that needed their "urgent attention." But we weren't convinced their reasons were always entirely real. Their exasperation at our feeble attempts to reproduce certain sounds was usually quite obvious, even though they tried hard to conceal it.

One night our landlord, Mr. Liban, gave us lots of words. His enthusiasm increased as we repeated most words well, until with great excitement he said, "I am very keen to see our

language in writing, and the children of the village learning to read our language."

However, as we struggled to mimic what to us seemed a grammatically complex word, but to him was simply another word, his enthusiasm appeared to diminish. Obviously irritated at our awkwardness, he suddenly stood up and declared, "Never mind, we'll cover it again later!" And then he quickly left us.

As we learned and analysed the language during those first few months, we found there were four vowels and 17 consonants, including what we call a "glottal stop." The glottal stop, a little catch of the breath in a word, has no sound, but its use can show the difference between my dog and another dog.

The glottal stop is easier to distinguish when it occurs at the end of a syllable. In writing it is indicated by a grave accent over the preceding vowel when it occurs at the end of a syllable, or a hyphen when it occurs at the beginning of a syllable, unless that syllable begins the word—in that case it's not shown at all. The only difference between *manyaman* and *manyam-an* is the slight catch of breath between "m" and "a" in the second word. In normal conversation, where words run into each other and sounds seem to overlap, it was almost impossible for us to notice the difference; but it was very important that we got it right. While *manyaman* means "to thank," *manyam-an* means "to destroy." When we talked of thanking God, we didn't want to say we were destroying God!

The words *manayaw* and *man-ayaw* also sound similar in normal speech, but using the right word is rather critical. If we had used *man-ayaw* instead of *manayaw* when we were talking about God, instead of saying, "Let's praise Him," we'd have said, "Let's take His head!" We would certainly have had everyone's attention.

The vowels in words like *kar* and *kor* had us tossed for a while. They both sounded exactly the same. It was a relief when we discovered they do sound the same. The context of the words revealed the separate meanings.

We had more fun with the "l" sounds. There are eleven distinct ways of pronouncing "l." One sounds just like the English "l" when it's used at the beginning of a word, or in the middle of a word if it begins a syllable but only if the previous letter is also an "l"—but even then the first "l" of the two sometimes sounds like "d," depending on the speaker.

If an "l" in the middle of a word is either preceded or followed by the "i" vowel, it sounds like the English "l." But if the vowel preceding it is one of the other three vowels—a, o and u—the "l" sounds a lot like an English "r"...but not quite. The tongue shoots forward to the front of the mouth for an instant.

There are several different "r"-like sounds, which would actually sound like "l" except for the particular vowels or consonants either side of it. In some contexts, it might sound like a real English "r," or a "backed r," where the front of the tongue is pulled towards the back of the mouth to make the sound. But those "r" sounds only occur at the end of syllables—the end of some syllables, that is. With some older speakers it sounds like a "y"...but not quite, and with younger speakers it sounds like a "j"...but not quite.

A lot can be said in a single Southern Kalinga word. In English there are only five or six different words derived from the root word "go." In Southern Kalinga, we found 87! Up to ten affixes can be added to the root word *oy* to change its meaning, ranging from *umoy,* "he goes," to *nangiyaiyayancha,* "the time that they were going somewhere, carrying something with them."

After six months, I asked one of the older men how we were progressing with the language. He commented, with no shyness or apology, "You speak as well as a five-year-old child." He smiled, as if he were being kind to us.

Well, we called it an airstrip!

In September 1974, history was made, in one more way than intended. It was the first time a plane ever landed at Mallango. It was also the first time a plane ever crashed at Mallango!

The 150 km trip by road from Bagabag to Mallango normally took three days, with a change of bus each day and long overnight stops. The average speed on the mountain roads was only 12 km/h, with a top speed of 20 km/h. In some places we could have gone faster, but we'd have had to walk. It used to take us two or three days to recover from the bus trip.

Flying would certainly be a better way to travel, as we would arrive at the village fresh and ready to begin work. An airstrip was therefore a necessity. We had one problem, however...there was no flat ground anywhere in those mountains.

A patch of grazing land just a few minutes' walk south of the village looked a remote possibility. Straddling the top of a ridge, it was impossible to irrigate for rice growing, so only grass grew there. With its steep, uneven surface, it was certainly not ideal for an airstrip, but it was the closest thing to ideal that we could see and it would need a lot of work to make it useable.

We presented our need to Kissub and the other village leaders. Not only would it benefit us, we explained, but it would also provide a way to get seriously ill people to hospital quickly.

Early one morning, over 100 people began digging and clearing what we hoped would become an airstrip. By noon it was finished, at least to our untrained eyes. It was 120 metres long—quite adequate for the Helio-Courier planes we would use. They were designed for short take-offs and landings.

The width was a little uneven—ten metres at its widest point and six at its narrowest. The two humps, looking like giant speed traps, bothered us a little. We hoped they wouldn't bother the pilots. Perhaps they wouldn't even notice them!

Chief pilot George Fletcher agreed to fly over for an aerial inspection as soon as he could. We prayed he would be impressed so that we could fly out to Bagabag at the end of the month rather than go by road, especially as Judith would be nearly eight months pregnant by then.

On the morning George came, we were waiting at the strip with 300 curious Mallango people, all eager to see their first plane up close. Gasps and cheers followed the plane as George flew the length of the strip, several metres of air safely separating him from the ground.

On his seventh pass, there was a deafening roar from everyone, and large lumps rose in our throats when the wheels touched the ground. We thought the plane was going to land, but it didn't. Instead, the engine suddenly roared, the plane soared off into the brilliant blue sky and it was soon out of sight.

Later, when I talked to George by radio, he said he had flown as low as he dared so he could see what might be expected during a real landing. The humps were a problem. They were too high. More work would have to be done to make the strip safe.

He gave instructions for improving it, but even after the workers reluctantly did all they felt was needed, it seemed only marginally better. We doubted George would approve.

Ten days later, George flew to Mallango again. This time Bill Powell, also a pilot, was with him. After circling three times, the plane's nose pointed at the lower end of the strip and it slowly approached, its engine almost silent. As it gently touched down, the engine roared again and the plane appeared to tiptoe unsteadily, like a lady holding her skirt up above her ankles to avoid puddles of water, as it rolled along the still uneven surface of the strip and stopped at the top. A perfect result.

The hundreds of spectators who had come from nearby villages chased the plane up the strip, eager to see it up close and touch it. After some of their curiosity was satisfied, everyone moved back off the strip again while Bill prepared to practise take-offs and landings. While George stood to one side of the strip to observe the plane's performance from the ground, Bill performed two perfect take-offs and landings. He then invited three men, including *barrio* captain Kissub, to take their first plane ride. They all agreed without hesitation. It would be something they'd tell their grandchildren about for years to come!

Everything seemed normal until Bill tried to land again. The plane came in low, rocking a bit as it approached the lower end of the airstrip. Just as the wheels touched the ground, Bill felt a gust of wind nudge the plane slightly off course. With very little ground space available, he quickly pulled on the throttle and the plane with its nervous-looking passengers soared upwards again.

On his next attempt, there was no wind so he set the plane down. Suddenly the left wing rose, lifted by a strong gust of wind rushing up the mountainside. The plane then abruptly dropped again. Kissub, sitting in the front passenger seat, looked out at us, his face silently pleading for help.

Bill pulled on the throttle, desperately attempting to take off again. But he was committed to a landing this time, and it careened from side to side, unable to lift off. Further fierce wind gusts forced it from one side of the narrow strip to the other as he struggled to regain control, without success.

There was no alternative but to try to stop, so he slammed his foot on the brake pedal with all the strength he could muster. The plane skidded towards the cliff edge near the top end of the strip and disappeared from sight.

We felt sick. There was an almost vertical drop of 400 metres. Frozen to the spot where we were standing, we listened for the sound of the plane crashing down the side of the hill, but we heard nothing. There was just an eerie silence.

We were quickly aroused to action when Judith remembered that moments before the crash George had been standing at the cliff edge, right in the path of the plane as it left the strip. Now there was no sign of him. As we ran towards the cliff, Judith shouted, "George!" I called out, "He must have been knocked over the edge."

Reaching the top of the strip, to our tremendous relief we saw both George and the plane, safe. The plane had stopped on a grassy slope just below the ridge. It was resting on one wing, just 30 centimetres from the drop into the valley below.

Everyone quickly clambered out. Bill looked shaken, but his passengers appeared fine. Kissub calmly stated, "It was no worse than some bus rides I've had. Three times I've been on buses that have fallen into a ravine."

Twenty men dragged the plane back up onto the strip where Bill and George inspected it carefully. The covering on the left wing was damaged, but not badly enough to ground the plane; the left stabiliser (the smaller rear wing), however, would have to be replaced. They called Bagabag, reported the bad news, and discussed plans to repair it.

Two of our colleagues, Winston Churchill and Dave Ohlson, left Bagabag by road early that afternoon with a generator, tools and a spare stabiliser. Meanwhile, George and Bill set to work pulling the rear section of the plane apart.

Winston and Dave arrived mid-morning the next day. They would have arrived earlier, but five kilometres before they reached the trail to Mallango, the engine of their Kombi van fell out onto the road. With a fence post holding the engine in place, they were soon on their way again to help with the repair job they had really come to do. It took the rest of the day to do that.

Next morning we bought a pig to butcher and distribute to thank the people for their help. The village people also contributed enough to buy another pig, and we all feasted and danced from dawn till dusk. The people loved any opportunity to celebrate.

Life, Death and Other Mysteries

The following day, George and Bill were able to take off for Bagabag. Since they weren't allowed to take passengers on a damaged plane, Judith, then nearly eight months pregnant, hiked to the road with our children to drive back to Bagabag with Winston and Dave. I decided to stay another week to get some more language data to work on, since we expected to be away for three months.

The pilots agreed that we could use the airstrip, but only if there was no wind—a condition not easily met.

From the village, I watched the van heading south until it was out of sight, and half an hour later, as I gazed longingly at the road, wishing I had gone with them, I saw it return and head north instead! I learned later that a landslide, which was expected to take three days to clear, had stopped them from taking the shorter route to Bagabag and had instead forced them to take the longer route.

Before the plane left, I remembered having joked to Dick Gieser a few weeks before about how we would like to live in a village about 3,000 feet above sea level. It would be impossible to gauge the altitude without an altimeter, of course, but Dick had said, "I'll see what I can do!"

A quick look at the plane's altimeter told us the altitude of the airstrip: 3,050 feet. With the village about 50 feet below the strip, that put Mallango almost exactly 3,000 feet above sea level. God had granted us even a cheeky little request like that.

Steven's birth

After a long, busy week of language work after my family left Mallango, I was more than ready to leave too. We would be back in two or three months, and several people assured me they would work on the airstrip in our absence so that the pilots would feel easier about landing there again.

After the apparently standard three-hour wait for a bus, it arrived already packed. But I wasn't going to let it leave

without me. I convinced the conductor that I had to get on.
I needed to get to my family.

Mallango people had very generously given me lots of gifts
to take to my family, including 30 pumpkins, 50 chokoes, a
variety of fruits and a good supply of coffee beans. So instead
of only one box, I had four to carry and wondered how
I would manage them all when I had to change buses.

I needn't have worried, however. At Bontoc I discovered
that during the four-hour trip from Mallango my load had
lightened significantly—the people riding on top of the bus
had eaten all the fruit. So, with only two boxes left to carry,
I reached the next town, Banaue, mid-afternoon to find there
were no more buses or jeeps going on to Bagabag that day.
I would have to stay the night at Banaue.

I booked into the Valgreg Hotel, which I later discovered
perches precariously on the edge of a cliff—if I had realised
just how precariously, I may have tried another hotel.

There was a choice of rooms—"room without bath" was
P5 (50 cents); "room with bath" was P7 (70 cents). I opted
for the luxury of the latter, only to find that the bath was a
30-gallon drum of very cold mountain water with an old
saucepan for a scoop. I skipped the bath. It was much too
cold. I had wasted P2.

Next morning, after only a couple of hours sleeping and
several hours slapping mosquitoes, I caught a minibus to
Bagabag, arriving a very happy man.

A week later, we all went to Manila. Our third child
was due any day. Colleagues Ron and Willie Grable
kindly offered us the use of their car and left spare keys
with us every night so that when Judith went into
labour, we could just jump in the car and go. It sat outside the
guesthouse every night—except the night we needed it.

On November 9, when Judith told me it was time to move,
I raced outside to start the car. It wasn't there! We heard later

that someone had borrowed it, just for that night. So I grabbed the key to the SIL van and within 15 minutes we were at the hospital.

Judith was convinced that the birth was imminent, but the receptionist wasn't. Before she would allow us any further inside the hospital, she insisted on filling out the admittance record in its entirety. She even needed to know Judith's mother's maiden name. Amazed, we asked why that particular information was needed. She had no idea. But there was a place to write it, so would we please tell her.

As Judith lay on the office floor, moaning in pain, the diligent receptionist continued to meticulously record Judith's life history, refusing to be distracted until her task was completed and carefully checked—in triplicate. Then she called for a wheelchair to transport Judith to a prenatal ward. Judith really didn't think she needed any more waiting time.

Mercifully, we met the doctor in the hallway. With just one glance at Judith's face, he ushered us into the delivery room and within two minutes Steven was born.

Little to enthuse

Two months later, I caught a bus back to Mallango to make sure the airstrip was ready and was disappointed to find that none of the extra work required by the pilots had been done. Everyone was too busy in their gardens. I sighed and tried to accept the delay, hoping some would soon be able to help.

Each morning I walked to the strip and chipped away at the humps, but the ground was like rock and it was difficult doing it alone. I had too much time to think about my family and how much I was missing them. The many children who accompanied me each day at least served to distract me momentarily from my misery. At night, to give me something else to occupy my mind, I worked at learning the language.

Once again it was difficult finding people willing to sit and teach me the language. It wasn't something they had ever done before we came, and they couldn't imagine why we would want to learn it.

A week after my return to Mallango, the airstrip was still unusable. It was so frustrating trying to get help. No one seemed willing. I was missing my family, and finding the language overwhelming. Sometimes I wanted to be alone, so I could at least have a good cry. But even that wasn't possible, except at night when everyone was asleep.

Emilio noticed how lonely I looked, and he dropped in to talk every morning and evening on his way to and from the school where he was the head teacher.

At last, on day eight, some men offered to work, and that night I went to sleep comforted by the assurance that the airstrip work would finally begin next morning.

I was woken before dawn by the sound of heavy rain on the iron roof. Normally I enjoyed that sound, as long as I was inside and the rain stayed outside, but not this time. Rain meant there would be no work done that day. The airstrip improvements would be set back yet another day, perhaps several, as with the much-anticipated rain people would want to take the opportunity of planting rice instead.

In my selfish misery, a poster on the wall caught my eye. It pictured a baby sitting in a high chair with an upturned bowl of spaghetti on his head. The text under it said, "This is the day the Lord has made. Rejoice and be glad in it!" I felt marginally better, happy to let God handle the situation. I certainly couldn't handle it.

That evening, content with their rice at last planted thanks to the rain, several men offered to work on the strip next day. In the morning, forty arrived with shovels and they tackled the biggest hump with great enthusiasm. Their enthusiasm waned as the morning wore on, however, with the ground so hard. The rain hadn't softened it at all.

Life, Death and Other Mysteries

Before noon, they stopped work, looked at me hopefully, and declared it was good enough. But my guess was that their "good enough" would still not be sufficient to satisfy the pilots, so I asked them to take just a little more off the biggest hump. With no attempt to hide a clear lack of enthusiasm, they slowly turned and tackled the hard earth again.

Next day, only 25 men turned up in the morning and 5 in the afternoon. Some brought rocks to place along the sides of the strip. They would give the pilot a reference point after he landed, as once the rear wheel was down, he couldn't see the ground in front of the plane. There were many others home in the village that day, but they didn't offer to help. Maybe they were tired of the whole thing. I was getting that way too.

On the third morning, when I had hoped the work would be completed, I awoke to news that a man had committed suicide during the night. One of our neighbours, unable to cope any longer with not being able to provide a better life for his poor family, killed himself by drinking insecticide. There would be no work done that day.

I was assured, however, that work would resume the following day. The normal period of several days' mourning would not be observed. By committing suicide, the man had brought shame on his family, so he was literally dropped into his grave within 24 hours. Two weeks later, the dead man's children were using his grave mound as a starter for their go-carts!

There was some good news that day. Judith told me on the two-way radio that Elizabeth had asked Jesus to come into her heart. Judith wasn't sure how much Elizabeth understood but thought she probably understood as much as any four-year-old could. After Elizabeth told Judith of her commitment to follow Jesus, she added, "I'm going to pray for Steven, because he hasn't asked Jesus to come into his heart yet." He was, after all, already three months old.

With a distinctly increased reluctance, a few joined me at the strip on the fourth day, and we worked hard at the humps again. But late in the afternoon, they put down their shovels and declared that they had done all they were prepared to do. Leaving them to gather up their tools, I walked slowly back to the village, feeling sure that the pilots would still not be satisfied but unable to ask the men to do anything further.

I learned later that although I paid the men wages for their work, I was unknowingly building up other debts with them. Because they had gone out of their way to do this work for us, they expected more than wages, and years later some were still reminding us of the work they had done for us and asking for financial help to send their sons or daughters to college. However, there was only so much that we could do with our limited resources. It was a part of the culture that we found very hard to adjust to.

When things came to a head...a chicken's head!

When I reached the strip next morning for another pondering look at what was and what might have been, I was startled to find a blood-soaked chicken's head on a pole at the bottom end of the airstrip. The pole was stuck in the ground to one side, with the chicken's head facing away from the strip.

There was no one else there, so I walked back down to the village for coffee and to ask about what I had found. Some of the men offered to tell me. A little bird they called the *ichaw,* or the "omen" bird, had flown across the strip just as the men were gathering up their tools the previous evening. And since that was considered a "bad omen," a hen had been killed and offered to the spirits, its blood sprinkled on the strip in the hope that it would prevent harm to anyone landing there in the future. Its head faced in the direction the ichaw bird had flown, "so that the bad omen would be taken away from the strip."

That reminded me of something I had seen the morning after the plane accident. I had asked about what looked like a large bloodstain near the spot where the plane had finished up but was told it was just the remains from a meal eaten by the watchers during the night. Now, hearing about the chicken head, my curiosity was aroused and I asked about that blood-stain again. Someone said, "At that time, a pig was offered to prevent further accidents on the airstrip. By the shedding of its blood, the evil was transferred to the pig."

As I tried to process in my mind what I was hearing, I suddenly had a great desire to tell them there was another way; if they trusted God to help them He would, and they wouldn't need to kill their animals in their uncertain desire that the spirits would treat them right. Then I realised they had done it for our well-being. They had done the only thing they believed would prevent harm to us, and it had cost them a lot. I told them I appreciated their concern for us.

A piece of the chicken meat was given to me, but I didn't feel like eating it—not yet. The idea of eating the flesh of animals offered to the spirits was something I would have to work through. I wondered, however, if that blood-soaked chicken's head might open the way for me to ask about the spirits. We had tried to bring the subject up several times, but the response was always, "Oh, that's just the superstitious belief of the old people. We don't believe that any more."

But we suspected they still did, and now with this episode clearly in everyone's minds, I decided I would ask about it again soon.

Two long weeks after my return to Mallango, Bill flew in to check the state of the airstrip. After five passes at different heights, he landed, coming to a rather cautious halt in barely 60 metres. After his previous experience, I admired him for trying again.

Bill seemed reasonably happy with the strip but wanted the rocks along the edges painted white for better visibility, and the lower end excavated a little more so that the first hump wasn't so steep at the point where the plane set down.

The strip would still be marginal, but useable. Then, after three more test take-offs and landings, he was gone again.

There's something about watching a plane flying away, getting smaller and smaller in the distance, and the feeling of loneliness it leaves when one is standing on a hillside surrounded by open space. There was no shortage of people— I was surrounded by them—but a vital ingredient in my life and experience was still missing. Next day, Bill returned with my precious family. Now I was ready to fully rejoice!

When babies are born

Early one morning we were woken by a man shouting outside. It was Charsin. It was the wedding of his sister, Ipin, that we had attended during our first week in the village. We still didn't know enough of the language to work out exactly what he was saying, but someone explained to us that Ipin, who was due to give birth to her first child within a few weeks, was ill and had lapsed into unconsciousness. "Evil spirits have taken her spirit away, as if she has died," we were told. Charsin was pleading with the spirits to return his sister's spirit and let her live.

After examining her, Judith felt confident that both mother and baby would survive if the baby could be induced. But her family was convinced she would die, and some men were already preparing to kill a water buffalo to feed the guests at her funeral.

"But she needn't die," Judith pleaded with the relatives. "If you will take her to the hospital, there's a good chance she will live, and the baby too." "But we have no transport," one replied, "and she can't be carried in her present condition."

We suddenly thought of the plane. If it could come, and her family would consent, Ipin could be taken to the Lutheran hospital at Abatan, only minutes away by air. There she would receive better attention than anyone in Mallango could possibly provide.

After some discussion, the family agreed. I ran to our house and called the pilot at Bagabag. When the plane came, Ipin, her husband and mother flew out, and within a couple of hours a beautiful baby girl was safely delivered. Grateful for such timely help, Ipin named her baby Judith.

A week later, after they returned to Mallango, we were invited to their home to eat rice cake. Entering the house, we noticed something unusual. There were three cooking pots upside down in the middle of the room, with grass around them; rope was strung across the room, and some objects were hanging from it; and a small plate of rice cake had been placed on a bamboo platform on the porch.

Two of the old men, Kissub and Marnawa, explained to us what it all meant. "This ceremony is called *kabfò,*" they said. "We do it for all newborn children." They went on to tell us how the ceremony is considered a thanksgiving celebration. All the relatives of the child's parents, and everyone in the village who wants to, come to join the parents in celebration. A shaman (spirit medium) chants the songs that are associated with the ceremony, and chickens and pigs are sacrificed.

"Do you have to do it?" we asked.

"It's very dangerous not to," Kissub assured us. "Once, when a family decided not to do it, the baby's leg became deformed. But as soon as the shaman was called and the *kabfò* ceremony was commenced, the child's leg was healed."

Cautiously pushing it a little further, I said, "When Steven was born, we didn't do all this. But nothing bad happened to him."

Marnawa nodded, and said, "Ah, but it's only we Kalingas who have to do it!"

We felt uncomfortable as we watched the shaman communicating with the spirits. We'd had no experience with evil spirits, and here we were witnessing an encounter with the spirit world by people who were obviously afraid of the spirits.

But as Judith and I watched what was to us a bizarre scene, something occurred to both of us. After all our doubts—not wanting to go there at first, feeling so much out of our comfort zone, understanding little of what was going on—we both suddenly had no doubt that this really was where God wanted us, as if He was saying to us, "You're in the right place. This is what I've been preparing you for. This is where I want you."

We looked at each other, and each seemed to know what the other was thinking. It was a good feeling!

Next morning, I woke up feeling sick. When I told old Singon I was sick, she laughed and with a twinkle in her eye said, "Would you like me to call the shaman for you? She has a way to make you well." I suddenly felt much better. When I told Singon I would be fine, we laughed together about it, but I didn't tell her that I found the incident more than a little unnerving.

A few weeks later, another couple had a baby son whom they named Bruce. Then two more baby girls were also named Judith, one of them the granddaughter of Ampug, the shaman. But when Ipin's baby died from an upper respiratory problem, the names of the other two Judiths were immediately changed! No more babies would be named Judith. And when baby Bruce also died, the potential for more babies named after me also ended.

David's TB

The next time we went out to our support centre at Bagabag, we took David to the clinic. He'd had a fever for several days and it hadn't responded to our treatment. X-rays showed he had primary complex TB. He would need to take medicine for at least 12 months.

We felt terrible. While carefully tending to all the medical needs of the villagers, we had failed to notice that one of our own children was sick. But we are thankful that his illness was discovered early and that it had no lasting effect.

Consistent language help

At last we felt we were doing fairly well learning the language. We'd had a succession of casual language helpers, but no one had the time, or more likely the patience, to spend a lot of time helping us. Part-time help was okay, but too often no one was available. To enable us to learn the language well and to get started on translation, we'd need consistent help. So I asked Kissub if he knew someone who might be able to work with us full-time.

Without hesitation, he said, "My nephew Saryong would be the best person to help you. But he's very busy."

We knew exactly where Saryong was at that moment—outside our house, digging the pit for our toilet. In his late thirties, Saryong and his wife Lùfay had five children. One of very few in Mallango to finish high school, Saryong had gone on to college but had to drop out after only one semester due to lack of money. Now he was a farmer like everyone else in the village.

He was also a good carpenter and had been recommended to us when we wanted some cupboards made. He had certainly done a very professional job. Since we had become weary of having to beat pigs off when we went to the "toilet" in the bushes, we had also asked him to install the water-seal toilet, which included digging a good-sized hole.

When I asked him if he would be willing to work for us, to help us learn the language and translate the Bible, he replied, "I have my fields to tend to, as I must provide for my family, but I will give you as much time as I can. We will begin as soon as I finish digging."

A few days later he accompanied us to Bagabag for a workshop to help us write up our discoveries about the sounds of the language.

As we walked from the hangar towards the three-bedroom house where we would stay for the next three weeks, Saryong asked, "How many families will be staying with us? Two more?" Hearing that we had the house to ourselves, he expressed surprise. He couldn't comprehend how such a big house could be just for us—it was about four times the size of his own.

As we worked together one night, I had a tape of gospel songs playing softly in the background. Saryong's command of English was good and he was obviously enjoying the songs. During one of them, "When the Roll is Called Up Yonder," he stopped working, put his pen down and listened intently. Curious, I also stopped working and watched him.

At the end of the song, he looked up and said, "That's the best song I've ever heard." He picked up the Living Bible that was on the table and started reading it. He was still reading it, seemingly oblivious to everything else that was happening around him, when I went to bed a couple of hours later.

At the breakfast table, Saryong ate quietly. As he finished, he looked up at us and said, "I have something to tell you."

Judith and I looked at each other. Had we done something wrong? Was he going to leave before we'd finished the workshop?

"I have decided to let others work my fields," he said, "so I can devote all my time to this work."

We were both relieved and delighted and wanted to hug him but since it wasn't culturally appropriate, we didn't. We told him how pleased we were about his decision. Later, Judith and I talked about the possible implications. While it was marvellous news, we were also concerned for Saryong. It would not have been an easy decision for him. He was giving up a lot, since by letting others manage his fields, his family would get only a share of the already small crop that his rice fields produced. I'll never forget Judith praying that night, "Lord, please, don't let us let him down!"

Medical treatment and mistreatment

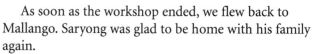

As soon as the workshop ended, we flew back to Mallango. Saryong was glad to be home with his family again.

During the next few days, a steady stream of people came wanting medical attention, so we didn't get much work done. Yet we were happy to provide simple medical help because it gave us a way of giving something back to the people for the hospitality they were showing us.

A trained nurse, Judith carried most of the medical load. Medical treatment was usually straightforward, but sometimes she found the responsibility overwhelming, particularly when she had to diagnose illnesses. I mainly handed out tablets and gave the odd injection. Adults preferred injections to tablets, insisting, "If it doesn't hurt, it can't be doing any good." But no one liked getting injections from me, even though my lack of skill in that area assured them of pain. They thought that since I was twice as heavy as Judith, my injecting would have twice as much force and therefore hurt too much.

One man who experienced my medical attention has possibly never forgotten it. He worked in a gold mine but had come home to recover from an infection. Judith was out visiting when he arrived from his village for the first of a series of penicillin injections, so I offered to give it. I was happy for the opportunity to get some practice.

Since there were many observers inside our house, he insisted the injection be given in his arm rather than his buttock. So I filled the syringe, sterilised his skin, and attempted to push the needle in. It wouldn't penetrate his mine-hardened muscle. A second attempt also failed. Then I stepped back, and holding the syringe like a spear I half threw, half guided it towards his shoulder. It bounced off.

Determined not to let it beat me, and by now almost oblivious to his discomfort and the observers' delight,

I placed the point of the needle against his skin and leaned on it. This time it penetrated, and with pain registering clearly on his face, the penicillin was injected. I probably shouldn't have been surprised to find, when I pulled the needle out, that it had bent about 80 degrees. All the observers were amused. The patient wasn't.

I never saw him again. I don't know what he did about the other nine injections he needed.

Later, a girl from another village came seeking medical help. Her hand was badly swollen from an infected cut on her palm and she wanted it lanced. Since Judith was out visiting again, I offered to do the job. I took a new razor blade, sterilised it over the gas flame, then carefully guiding it through her almost closed hand to the inflamed area, I made a neat slit. An indescribable mess gushed out of the wound. The girl fainted! Fortunately, she was caught by the other women who were jammed into our tiny porch. Quick breaths of fresh air helped me to stay upright.

As the women held her unconscious body, they screamed at Saryong, the only other man present, to call out to the spirits and beg them to return her spirit, believing that if they didn't she would die. But Saryong refused. Instead, he told them what he had been learning through reading the Bible. Surprisingly, their attention was distracted from the plight of the poor girl and they listened rather than insist he do what they had asked.

While he was talking, the girl regained consciousness and left quickly for her home. I never saw her again either.

THREE
Fun Times and Difficult Times

The beginning of something beautiful

E ach year at Easter, the Balangao Bible Church
held a Bible Conference, and invited people
from all nearby mountain groups. The
Balangao believers wanted others to have exposure
to the Gospel message too. Four Mallango men, including the
village leader Kissub, accepted their invitation to attend.

Although they didn't speak the Balangao language, they
would understand enough to get by. One of the reasons they
wanted to go was the opportunity it provided of visiting a village they'd never been to before, but the main reason was that
they would get to fly in the plane.

On their return, they all said, "The conference was wonderful!" We asked Kissub what it was all about, and he replied,
"It was about Jesus Christ from start to finish."

Emilio was impressed too. "There were delegates from lots
of other mountain groups too," he reported, "and we were all
treated by the Balangaos as friends. We were all impressed by
the followers of Jesus. They treat each other as if they are really
brothers and sisters. I cannot find words to describe it."

All four were particularly impressed by the good behaviour
of Balangao children, the hospitality of their host families, the
number attending the meetings, and the testimonies of the
believers. "This is something we'll never forget," they said.
They were keen to go again.

Fun Times and Difficult Times

"Lord, please make barking dogs mute!"

I wasn't surprised that Emilio was startled when he
heard his name called. It was well after dark, and when someone walked around outside at night, the dogs barked—always,
and without exception. The only time they didn't bark at
intruders in the village night was when those intruders were
spirits. Somehow, the dogs would recognise them and they
would whine softly and scurry under a house, tails between
their legs.

No one walked the whole length of the village at night without a canine musical accompaniment. Until the night I did it.

Steven, then eight months old, used to revel in the freedom
of his "walker," a seat with wheels in which he scooted around
the floor. We were always very careful to latch the makeshift
gate at the top of the stairs, but on this particular day the
child of colleagues visiting us left it open, and the invitation
to explore was too great to ignore.

We knew about the mistake when we heard his cry as he
tumbled down the wooden stairs, followed by the sickening
crack as his head hit the concrete step at the bottom. An
enormous lump instantly blossomed near his left temple.

We watched him closely all afternoon, and the lump
seemed to reduce a little. But around dusk his temperature
began to rise sharply. It quickly reached 40ºC, so we gave
him aspirin, sponged him with cold water, and prayed.

By 10 p.m. we were really worried. His temperature was
unchanged, and he was obviously in pain. As we prayed,
Emilio's name came to my mind and I said to Judith,
"How about if I go and ask Emilio to pray, too?" "Good
idea," she said.

Our house was near the bottom end of the village while
Emilio's was at the top-end, a good five minutes' walk for me
in daylight. It was pitch-black now. I set off nervously, flashlight in hand. Stumbling along cautiously, I waited for the first
of 100 dogs to begin disturbing everyone's sleep. No one went

48

outside after dark because the spirits were too active then, and if I was heard, and I had no doubt that I would be, the dogs would bark and people would be frightened. So I prayed, "Lord, I don't want to alarm anyone. Please keep the dogs quiet. Please make barking dogs mute!"

Apart from my footsteps, the clearest sound I could hear was my own breathing. I passed Charsin's house, the one with the most ferocious dog in the whole village, without hearing so much as a soft growl. I was utterly amazed.

I shone the flashlight all around me, bewildered. Canine heads were raised and sniffing in every direction—some on porches, others on the ground. Not one made a sound.

At last I reached Emilio's house. Standing on his steps, my heart pounding, I came face to face with Emilio's dog. I expected pandemonium to break out. Instead, it sat quietly on the doormat, staring at me.

I couldn't understand what was happening. I wanted to shout, "Come on! What's the matter with you? You're supposed to be protecting Emilio and his family! You're supposed to be barking!" And then I realised that God had answered my prayer and made all the dogs mute that night!

I called out to Emilio and he woke up, startled at hearing a voice outside. His first thought was, "Why isn't our dog barking? It must be a spirit calling my name!"

I called again, "Emilio! It's Bruce! I need your help." Recognising my voice now, he opened the door cautiously, and his appearance changed from alarm to relief. Ushering me inside, he asked, "What's wrong?" I told him about Steven's fever and asked him if he would pray for Steven. Although it struck me as odd that I would even ask him, since he hadn't ever indicated that he was a believer, I wasn't surprised when he agreed to pray. And he wasn't even curious about my reason for asking him in particular to pray.

On my return journey to our house, still no dogs barked, although I did hear the softest of whimpers from Charsin's dog.

Fun Times and Difficult Times

At 2 a.m., Steven's fever suddenly broke and he slept. We all did.

Later that day we heard the sequel to my late-night adventure. The whole village had heard about it. Everyone was amazed about the lack of reaction from the dogs.

What amazed us even more was Emilio's comment when he dropped in to see us that afternoon. "What you did last night," he said, "walking right through the village with not one dog barking, not even my own, so impressed me that I read the Bible and prayed for Steven until 2 a.m. Then I felt it was okay to go to sleep."

The impact continues

At Saryong's request, we began studying the Bible together. We studied for about two hours most days, sometimes three or four, before we started on the day's language or translation work. He asked lots of questions, many of them difficult to answer—but we found answers in the Bible to all of them. Again and again Saryong expressed amazement at our findings.

It was obvious to Judith and me that God was working in Saryong's heart and mind. We felt further encouraged when he asked if we could extend our Bible study to Sundays too, so that others could come and listen as well. We agreed to, of course, and he invited some others to join us the following Sunday. No one came.

The next time we were due to go to Bagabag for a workshop, it looked like the weather would prevent us leaving by plane. It had been raining heavily for several days, and the night before we planned to leave, someone said to Elizabeth, "It will be raining too hard in the morning. The plane won't be able to come."

Elizabeth, nearly five years old, promptly responded, "Yes, it will, 'coz me and Mummy prayed!"

Next morning at dawn, the rain stopped. I tried several times to call Bill on the radio to give him our good weather report, but he didn't respond. Instead, we heard him calling us, asking about the weather around Mallango and telling us it was raining hard in Bagabag. He told us later that even though it was raining there, he had decided to try to get us anyway, hoping that for some strange reason the weather would be clear over Mallango. The closer he got to Mallango, however, the rougher the turbulence became and the more he thought about turning back. But although he didn't understand why, he kept coming, even though he couldn't even hear us.

The instant he crossed the ridge and Mallango came into view, he flew into clear weather. As he was making his approach to land, however, light drizzle began falling on the plane's windscreen, but that wasn't going to stop him now.

We were all delighted to see the plane land, especially Elizabeth.

Saryong believes

A few days later, Saryong joined us at Bagabag. One morning at breakfast he announced to us, "I have been reading the Bible, and I understand it. What must I do now?"

Judith and I were delighted! We looked at some Bible verses with him and talked to him about believing in Jesus, but he said he wanted to talk with some others first. He began attending an early morning Bible study with men from other language groups, and a week later he trusted Jesus as his Savior.

Soon after the workshop ended, we returned to Mallango to find Saryong's two-year-old daughter Junel sick. Although we tried treating her with antibiotics, she showed no improvement at all but instead became weaker. A lot of pressure was put on Saryong to offer a sacrifice to the spirits, but he refused. When Junel's condition deteriorated even further, he was accused by relatives and neighbours of not caring about his little girl. That was very hard for Saryong to hear because he loved his family.

When Junel became unconscious, her mother, Lùfay, without Saryong's knowledge, called the shaman. The shaman determined that Junel's spirit had been taken by spirits who lived in a certain tree in the forest. They would release it if Lùfay was to take her there and offer a chicken.

That evening, Saryong arrived home from getting firewood to find dozens of people outside his home, and Lùfay leaving with Junel in her arms. He asked her where she was taking the child. When she explained what the shaman had advised, Saryong refused to let her go. "Wait!" he said. "I believe she will get well without a sacrifice."

Then he turned to me and said, "I'm going to ask God to heal our child, and then everyone will know that God is more powerful than the spirits, and you will pray with me."

In the next few seconds, a lot of thoughts went through my mind: Junel was dying; Saryong had made his bold statement in the presence of dozens of people, declaring he would trust God in the face of this onslaught from the spirits. If Junel died, people would conclude that God was less powerful than the spirits. What would that mean for our future? They certainly wouldn't be interested in what we were doing there.

I didn't have time to voice any of my hesitations because Saryong started praying. After he finished, I prayed too and then shuffled slowly back to our house to talk and pray with Judith and to ponder together what the future might hold for us there. I fully expected that the child would die.

Judith had a thought. "Let's try to get Junel to swallow some worm medicine. It wouldn't do her any harm and might just help her." We took some to her house, and her parents helped her to swallow the liquid, though she hardly had the strength even to do that.

Early next morning, Judith and I shuffled nervously towards Saryong's house, dreading what we would find inside.

Entering, we were overjoyed to see Junel sitting on the floor, eating. Her mother was holding her and asking Saryong about his faith.

I won't describe here the results of the medication. Maybe it was the worm medicine that had made Junel turn the corner. Maybe it was God who had healed her. Whatever had happened to make Junel well, we knew that God was involved.

Interference

Around midnight one night we were woken by the unmistakable sound of a pig being killed. It was a sound we hated because we knew it meant someone was sick and a sacrifice was being offered.

The noise came from the direction of Lakinchay's house. We knew he was sick, but didn't believe he was bad enough to warrant an animal sacrifice. I lay there thinking about the old man for a while and then, unable to sleep, decided to go and see what was happening. Dozens of men were sitting around outside his home, talking while they waited for a share of the meat from one of the huge pigs that Lakinchay's family had butchered.

I climbed the steps and went inside. Lakinchay was sitting close to the kitchen fire, surrounded by relatives. Looking up at me, his face expressing hopelessness, he whispered, "I'm dying."

It was hot inside the house and he was sweating profusely. Surprised to see he was wearing several layers of clothing, I exclaimed, "Why are you wearing all those clothes?" Looking at me perplexed now, he replied, "I want to look my best when I die!"

I suspected he only had an ulcer, which was probably so painful that he thought he was dying. "You'll die, all right," I suddenly blurted out, "if you don't get some of those clothes off!" Everyone was startled at my outburst—including myself. Lakinchay immediately took off most of his clothes.

Fun Times and Difficult Times

I wasn't quite sure what to do next but gave him some medicine that I hoped would help him. Then I sat with him for a couple of hours before going home, exhausted.

I tossed and turned the rest of the night, unable to sleep, feeling uncomfortable about what I had done. Lakinchay may have died, and maybe I shouldn't have interfered. After all, he was an old man. He was being well cared for by his family and he was ready to die. Since he didn't know the Lord, I couldn't just stand by and let him die without doing anything.

Around dawn I went to see him again. He was looking much better, and with a big grin he said to me, "I'm not going to die after all!"

His relatives, however, were not as happy as he and I were, and they let me know about it in no uncertain terms. "Why did you have to interfere?" they demanded. "Last night, we spent a lot of money on animals to honour the old man. But now he's going to live, and when he does eventually die, we'll have to spend more money for more animals."

Lakinchay sat quietly listening to their comments, saying nothing. No one asked him for his opinion. I decided this was not the time for me to ask him either.

In trouble again

There were other ways I surprisingly found myself in trouble too, although I pleaded ignorance each time. One involved the way I cleared my throat before speaking in public. I was often asked to speak at special functions since I was a guest in the village. (Judith was also a guest, but women didn't normally speak in public.) On such occasions I had a nervous habit of always needing to clear my throat before speaking. I did it as nicely as I could, with my hand covering my mouth, since I didn't want to risk offending anyone. I had no inkling, however, of the way my extreme care was received.

On one occasion after I finished speaking, a lady suddenly appeared in front of me, glaring and shaking a finger at me. She shouted angrily, "You really despise us, don't you?"

I was shocked by her outburst. "Why do you think that?" I asked sheepishly.

"When you clear your throat, you don't spit!" she shouted. "By not spitting, you are telling us that you despise us. You also tell us that when you yawn. You hide it from us with your hand. Why do you despise us so much?"

I was shocked at her unexpected outburst, and it took me a few seconds to grasp what she was saying. So that's why people always spat so energetically before speaking. It had seemed a pretty disgusting habit to me, particularly when pieces of betel nut and other colourful stuff shot in my direction. And here I was, exercising my Western social graces by covering my mouth whenever I yawned and by not spitting in public.

I quickly learned this lesson in Kalinga culture, however, and quite enjoyed the local methods of loud, musical yawning and hearty spitting.

Fun—at my expense

The village's meagre water supply was frequently cut when a water buffalo stepped on the narrow pipe and broke it. One time I was invited to accompany the men to the source, 8–12 km away, to fix it. It was to prove more than exercise and friendship-building for me.

As we set off, Juanito, a schoolteacher, handed me a large green leaf. "It's a special leaf," he said. "You should put it in your pocket. It's something that old people carry to make a long journey like this more comfortable."

I was in yet another quandary. Was this something to do with the spirits, perhaps to ensure their protection? I didn't want to offend anyone again, but I was just a little wary about the signal I might be giving the men. Would I be agreeing with their beliefs about the spirits if I did as he said? However, with a quick, silent prayer for wisdom and protection from the Lord, I put it in my pocket. Juanito seemed pleased.

About two hours later, looking quite serious, he asked me for the leaf. I wondered why he wanted it. As I handed it cautiously to him, he grinned and said, "I want to defecate, and I need the leaf to wipe my backside afterwards."

I stood there speechless, not really comprehending what I was hearing, and then feeling my face becoming red and warm as I realised he'd set me up. As he walked away, he burst out laughing and added, "Thanks for being so neighbourly and carrying it for me since I have no pocket!" Everyone else laughed too. I wanted to tell him exactly what I thought of him and his crude joke but kept my thoughts to myself. I saw the bright side of it too and decided it was probably good that they felt so comfortable with me that they could joke like that with me. Years later Juanito was still reminding us about his trick and my gullibility.

We had much to learn about Kalinga culture. The people are so much a part of their culture, influenced by it as much as they are by their parents. Their land, their legends, their language—their culture is their life.

People believed that the spirits would cause a man to have boils if he said the name of his mother-in-law. No one would intentionally say her name, but we saw many terribly painful examples of obvious slips of the tongue.

From time to time, I would be asked the name of my mother-in-law. I could tell from their cheeky grins that they were just joking, but I decided not to tell them anyway. And each time I was left feeling in a bit of a quandary. By not say-ing my mother-in-law's name, was I in fact inadvertently telling them that I was afraid of the spirits just like they were? On the other hand, if I did tell them her name, would I be foolishly throwing out a challenge to the spirits?

One day I decided to tell people, as a way of showing them that the spirits had no power over me. I was a child of God.

There would be no risk to me. I was telling a group that Judith's mother was planning to visit us soon, and someone asked with a grin, "What's her name, Bruce?" Everyone laughed, sure that I wouldn't answer. Several others joined in the game and asked me too. After a few minutes' banter, I shrugged my shoulders and said, "Her name is Doris."

Within 24 hours, to my dismay but to the delight of many others, I had two large, very painful boils on my neck—plainly visible to everyone and painfully evident to me—and in the week that followed another seven appeared on my body! Everyone joked about the reason I had boils. Judith and I tried to explain how it was just an unfortunate coincidence, but Kalingas don't believe in coincidence. We began to wonder about it too.

Five years later another batch of boils reared their ugly heads, as it were, and in the three years that followed I had a total of 80. And I didn't say my mother-in-law's name once! However, although the most painful were either on or inside my nose, I felt I was indeed fortunate not to have more than two at a time. When one was right on the end of my nose, I asked Elizabeth what my nose looked like and she said, "Ayers Rock."

Various parts of my anatomy were also the object of much fun among the people. The children's description of my bald head: "Your forehead is like an airstrip." The way they observed my stomach, which sometimes assumed the shape of a "spare tyre": "The water tank is overflowing!" Other things they said of me can't be written here out of my respect for the reader.

Other jolts

While I was transmitting at roll call on the two-way radio one morning, lightning struck the antenna and the jolt flung my arm back. Judith was shocked to see me throw the mike at her, or at least for a quick second that appeared to be what I was doing. With my other hand I hastily disconnected the antenna, and then just as hastily, I explained my actions to her. I was sore all down my left side for several days afterwards.

One event that was to become clearly etched in our memories was the first time Ken Kruzan made a mail drop over our airstrip. He had carefully boxed the 62 items to be delivered and very kindly offered to drop the box out the door of the plane on his way further north. He had done it for others dozens of times, and we were starving for news from home so were grateful for his offer. He flew just above the airstrip as slow as he dared. He was a little higher and going a little faster than he'd planned, and instead of landing in just one place the mail landed in 62 places. The box broke open on impact, scattering its contents in many directions. One of the items was a clock. Time stood still that day—the clock never worked again.

FOUR

Another World

Fear of the spirits

Mallango is one of twelve villages that make up the Southern Kalinga language group. Stretched along the top of a steep, narrow ridge, the village is virtually impregnable to warring neighbours—but not to spiritual forces.

Because we had never been consciously involved with the spirit world before going to the Philippines, nor did we want to be particularly, we knew almost nothing about it. So when we found ourselves wrestling with spiritual forces in Mallango, our lack of understanding sometimes left us feeling bewildered.

Kalingas knew about the spirit world from bitter experience, and felt enslaved by it. We knew that if we were to have a successful ministry amongst them, we would have to learn about the spirit world from their perspective.

We weren't living with them long before we discovered that life for them was hard. They often saw their children die in infancy, unable to do anything to help them "because that's what the spirits had decided would happen."

Sacrificing their animals kept them poor. The spirits never seemed satisfied even when a family was completely destitute. Even after all their animals had been killed, their child might still die, their crops might fail, or some other misfortune might befall them. They lived in a constant state of bondage to an unseen yet very real host of malevolent spirits who controlled their lives.

Another World

In traditional Kalinga culture, most spirits are believed to be the wandering souls of the dead. If not appeased correctly, they may look for ways to harm the living. Every facet of life involves the spirit world in one way or another, and this involvement often causes them great distress.

Sickness, untimely death and all other adversities are generally attributed to the spirits. At birth, during childhood, while planting and harvesting, before hunting—either for animals or (mostly in the past) for heads—or for any other significant event, specific rituals have to be performed. These usually involve the sacrifice of chickens, pigs or even water buffaloes. To disregard even the slightest command of the spirits is to provoke vengeance.

Once when a child was sick, the shaman said the cause was something to do with the placement of the family's rice field and vegetable garden which faced each other across a brook. The father had to go to the garden twice and sacrifice a hen each time.

When Karnao's elderly father was sick, Karnao butchered a pig and the whole village came to a standstill while people came to visit and eat. Early one morning the old man dreamed that his soul left him, so someone yelled to the spirits to return it. They then butchered a water buffalo to appease the spirits. Someone said, "This is our medicine; we don't go to hospitals." However, they also asked us to give him an injection and he recovered.

Some women wear a snake skeleton on their head to protect them from lightning and thunder while they're working in their gardens. A cord is put around the waists of babies to protect them from serious illness. When a fellow killed an enemy, his family offered five pigs to appease the spirits so that no harm would befall the murderer or his family.

The day after a burial, no one goes to work in their fields, believing that if they do their crops will be destroyed by pests.

We heard of incidents of people who had been controlled by spirits. Most were women, and each had a different experience. One woman went outside her house every night and talked to spirits. When the spirits' demand for a pig sacrifice was apparently met, she recovered and hasn't been possessed since. Another woman, about to deliver a child, was forced by a spirit to stand up all night, which was very difficult for her. The spirit stopped tormenting her only when chickens were offered in a sacrifice.

Many times we witnessed the anguish of parents, even in the middle of the night, as they searched for someone willing to sell them a pig that met the spirits' requirements, and the urgency as they killed it, hoping that the spirits might spare their seriously ill child. We got to the stage where, if we knew someone in the village was sick, we found it hard to sleep, dreading the sound that might wake us during the night.

Two men sleeping outside the house of a man who had committed suicide woke feeling hands around their throats choking them. Fumbling for their flashlights, they switched them on only to find no one else there. The whining of their dogs indicated to them the presence of spirits. It was believed the spirit of the dead man was looking for his wife to do her harm. When it couldn't find her because she and the children were not sleeping in their house, it attacked the men sleeping outside instead.

One day I met a man of about 60 on the road between Mallango and Manangol. He was carrying a dead hen in a large clay pot. He had been to Mallango where, with the shaman's help, he had sacrificed it. I was told later that while the man had been working in his vegetable garden, the ichaw bird had flown over his head. He therefore had to offer a hen to the spirits so that he wouldn't die. The life of the hen was offered in his place.

The reality and power of the spirits were vividly illustrated in an incident involving a man from the village of Sumachor.

Another World

Needing new posts for his house, Felipe was cutting trees in the forest when he heard his name called. Looking around, he saw no one else there, so he kept working. A little later he heard the voice again. "Felipe," it said, "you must bring a big pig here and give it to us in exchange for the trees you are taking from our forest."

Felipe called out, "But I'm a poor man. I have no pig, not even a small one." But the demand was repeated, this time with the added threat, "If you disobey us, you will die!"

Shaking, Felipe sat down and thought about what he had just heard. Was it real or was he just hallucinating? The work was tiring, the sun was hot, and he had hiked a long way from his home. He stood up, saying to himself, "No, this is not really happening. It's just my imagination. I'm tired from all my hard work. My mind is playing tricks on me."

Looking around cautiously, he could still see no one. "My house needs repair," he muttered. "I can't waste time. I must keep cutting."

He bent down to turn the log he was working on. It wouldn't move. That was strange; it had turned easily before. Lifting his head to look along the log, he was startled to find people sitting on it. There were five, and the face of each one was a mirror image of his own.

He realised instantly that they were spirits. Grabbing his axe, he fled from the forest terrified. He shared his experience with the other villagers but knew he couldn't expect any help from them. He also knew he would never be able to meet the spirits' demand for a pig.

However, he still needed timber to repair his house and couldn't afford to buy it. So a week later, having experienced no repercussions from what he had already done in the forest, he decided to go and quickly collect just the trees he had already cut down. Perhaps the spirits would permit that. They could keep the rest.

Ten days later, searchers found his body at the bottom of a gorge.

Our little friend Ambet

Ambet lived a few houses from us. We remember her pretty little face with its cute smile. She had all the boundless energy of any eight-year-old and loved to carry her baby brother around on her back while their parents were busy in their fields. She also loved to come and stand outside our window and watch us work. Lots of children did.

Occasionally, Ambet wasn't among the little band of onlookers. Since she was one of our favourites, we would ask where she was.

One morning when she was absent, no one answered our questions regarding her whereabouts. The children just looked at each other without comment. We sensed that something was wrong. When we asked again, one of the older children came closer and whispered, "Ambet is sick. They say she's dying."

Ambet dying? Please, God! No!

The death of children was more common in Mallango before we arrived on the scene. Infant mortality had been around 60 percent with most deaths occurring between the ages of two and ten years. Simple treatment with aspirin, penicillin and worm tablets stemmed the sad tide, and only a handful died while we were there. The death of a child brought a blanket of grief over the whole village and also over us.

Grabbing our small medical kit, we rushed to Ambet's house hoping we could do something but fearing we were too late. Scrambling up the steps, we entered the dark interior and saw Ambet surrounded by her family and relatives. She was lying on a mat, unconscious. Everyone was sobbing. We joined them in their anguish.

Sitting near Ambet's head was old Tammù, a shaman. She was muttering something quietly while stroking the little girl's forehead with a leaf. It was the *chawà* healing ritual. We sat quietly watching as Tammù talked to a spirit familiar to her, trying to ascertain the cause of Ambet's illness and whether the spirits would accept anything for her recovery. If they said she would die, there would be no hope. She would die.

We remembered being told earlier about Ambet's birth. It had been such a happy occasion. Her parents already had five sons but they also wanted a daughter. Having many children was not a problem to Kalingas, even though most were poor. They accepted that at least half their children would probably die, so they had at least twice as many as they really wanted.

Along with the joy that followed birth was a period when special caution had to be exercised. So when Ambet was born, her parents carefully observed rituals passed down from their ancestors, which included certain restrictions on the activities of the family and the strict observance of food taboos.

No one dared ask why they should observe the rituals. They just knew they must. Since baby Ambet was unable to protect herself, she was vulnerable to the unwanted attention of evil spirits if the rituals were not strictly followed.

Ambet's oldest brother cooked rice, which was taken to the shaman to pray over. After her mother ate a little of the rice, the rest was shared by her family. That night her father butchered two hens as a sacrifice, and the following morning two more.

Certain taboos were also observed by Ambet's family. Even before she was born, her parents were not permitted to hunt or hold monkeys, snakes, lizards or turtles. If they held a monkey, for instance, Kalingas believed that their child would in some way resemble that creature when she was born. One little girl in Mallango was born with thick hair remarkably like monkey fur on part of her face. We were told that when her mother was pregnant she had held a monkey.

Many foods could not be eaten for a certain period, including pork, beef, cow's milk, eel and dog meat. Saryong told us that no member of a newborn baby's family would even consider touching meat for several weeks after the baby's birth until the kabfò ritual ceremony for newborn babies was performed. Even then they would not eat any meat until the baby "tasted" it first. A piece of meat only had to be put to the baby's lips and that qualified as tasting.

Kalingas believed that if a newborn baby's father ate pork without the baby tasting it first—even if he was away from the village at the time of the birth and didn't know his child had been born—fluid resembling pig's blood would flow from the baby's mouth until it died.

Saryong recalled walking through the village soon after the birth of his first child and catching the sweet smell of pig cooking. "Although my stomach craved pork," he said, "I immediately turned and hurried away. The consequences of disobeying the spirits were too terrible to risk. I was certain that if I ate any of the meat my daughter would die."

All of this had seemed quite bizarre to us, but what we did understand at that moment was that little Ambet was sick and probably dying.

Judith looked around at the blank faces and asked, "Why hasn't someone taken her to the hospital? It's only a four-hour hike away!"

"We don't know which spirit caused her sickness nor why," her father replied. "Even if we take her to the hospital and she's cured there, she'll just get sick again when we bring her back here."

Their fatalism disturbed us deeply, but all we could do was watch as Tammù, the shaman, performed her ritual. After several minutes she looked up. The sobbing and chattering ceased. "The spirits have told me that Ambet stole fruit from a tree near the brook," she reported. "They are demanding a pig in exchange for her life."

"A pig?" gasped her mother. "But we're poor! We have no pigs, and we haven't enough money to buy one." The shaman sat impassively. "Must it be a pig?" pleaded her father. There was no reply.

The devoted parents knew there was no alternative. A pig had to be bought and killed or their child would die. To enable them to buy one, her mother would have to sell some of her precious beads, family heirlooms handed down through several generations. That would add more pain to what she was already experiencing.

Slowly her mother stood up, made her way through the throng of relatives, and blinded by her tears, stumbled out of the house. We heard her speaking in urgent tones to her brother outside.

A few minutes later a squealing pig tied to a bamboo pole was carried into the front yard. Ambet's father sharpened a piece of bamboo, shaping it into a blade. Then he plunged it deep into the chest of the pig until a spurt of blood signified that its heart had been pierced.

Emitting ear-piercing shrieks, the pig continued to kick and struggle until its throat was slit. Then a couple of men lifted it by the back legs to allow the blood to drain into a bowl. That would be cooked and eaten later along with the rest of the meat.

Some of the men had started a fire, and now two of them slung the carcass over the flames to singe its hair. An acrid, sickly smell filled the air as the bristles crackled and shrivelled in the intense heat. Then Ambet's father slit open the pig's stomach, cut out the liver and gall bladder, and rushed inside the house to give them to the shaman. He sat down beside his wife to await the judgment of the spirits.

The shaman carefully examined the items. If they were an odd colour or an abnormal shape, she would know the spirits had not accepted this offering and another would be demanded.

Tammù slowly raised her head. "The spirits have accepted your offering," she announced.

The price had been high for her parents, but they were relieved. "Surely now the spirits will let our little girl live," her mother said, but everyone knew there was no guarantee that they would.

Ambet died that night. For the next two days her tiny body was seated on a makeshift bamboo chair in the house. Visitors came, shed tears, gave small gifts of money or food to her parents, and left. The gifts were carefully recorded so that Ambet's parents could return the favour when someone else's child died.

Her death seemed so unfair. Her parents had done all that was demanded of them, and still it wasn't enough. The burial was conducted quietly by her parents. Only close relatives were there as they gently placed her body in a shallow grave beside their house. We cried with Ambet's family and have many times since then (including now as I write about her) as we remember her.

Other children would also die. Not long after Ambet's death, a young boy named Kara became ill. The shaman said that the spirits of his grandparents had caused his illness because he had stolen some coffee from a neighbour's tree. Kara denied the charge. His father, who was openly antagonistic toward us and the work we were doing, was away at the time, so someone went to call him. While Kara's mother waited for her husband to return, she let Judith treat her son with an antibiotic. Judith also prayed for him.

That afternoon as we sat in their home preparing to give Kara another injection, his father arrived. He walked straight past us to his motionless child and began to wail, "*Anako. Anako.* (My child. My child.)" When Judith asked him if she could give Kara the injection, he turned and said angrily, "I don't want you to give my boy any more injections. Leave us alone! We have our own customs. We'll offer a pig and if the spirits are satisfied with that, they will leave us alone. If not, then the boy will die. If that's his fate, nothing can change it."

Another World

Kara died six hours later. Once again the Kalinga people were reminded of the frailty of life and the vulnerability of their own children in a world made hostile by spirits that sought to harm them.

Sad endings

Needing a break, we caught a bus to Bontoc about 50 km south for a weekend away from the village. On our return trip to Mallango, the guard on the bus was a police sergeant. A middle-aged man with nine children, he lived in Bangad, the village on the river down below Mallango.

A week later the bus was ambushed and the sergeant was shot dead. He had been well respected in his community, but by dying in such a violent way he had "shamed his relatives." He was therefore buried within 24 hours, without the long wake usually observed for adults of his status. His bullet-riddled, bloodstained clothes were not even changed, and as his coffin was being lowered into the grave, it was turned over so that he faced downwards. We were told that by facing away from the people he took his shame with him.

Another man committed suicide by stabbing himself. His body was dropped unceremoniously into a crudely dug grave. We could not understand the harshness of the treatment some people were accorded, but no one appeared to share our concern, or at least to express themselves in the same way as us. To Kalingas, what they did was simply their way of coping with what they regarded as profound shame.

Death is part of life for Mallango people. When an old person dies, people come from all around to pay their respects. If he was a peace pact holder, many will come from the other village in the pact. Each family in the deceased's village will supply rice and vegetables while the family provides the meat.

It's a happy occasion because the person has lived a long life, but it can be very expensive. The children of the deceased take turns providing and butchering a carabao, one per day until each has given one. Before the body is buried, it is usually seated on a bamboo chair in one corner of the house, dressed in new clothes and wrapped in a new blanket. The day after the burial no one goes to work in their fields, believing that if they do, their crops will be destroyed by pests.

Someone said it would be good if Mrs. Liban's father died while we were there because he was old and greatly respected and we would be able to witness the way he would be honoured. Since he was present when the statement was made, we looked at him, wondering what he thought about that. He smiled and agreed it would be good.

Spirit mediums and their gifts

Most of the spirit mediums, or shamans, in Kalinga are older women. Tammù was the main village shaman when we first went to Mallango. She had been appointed to her role by spirits. Her sister, Ampug, also a shaman, was self-appointed, though we never found out how she did that. Their "call," however, was recognised by everyone since they exhibited certain behaviour that proved they had been summoned by the spirits to assume the role of a medium.

Like Tammù and Ampug, most of the shamans were "general practitioners." They performed their ritual for anyone who asked for their services. A few, however, claimed specific gifts and specialised in healing only certain ailments. Their techniques were different. One could cure a headache by just breathing on the patient. Another could cure stomach pains with just a touch of the fingers. They passed their gifts of healing on to others by breathing on the one designated by the spirits to inherit the gift.

Another World

The omen bird

Spirits manifest themselves in many forms. We heard more about the ichaw, or "omen bird," after the airstrip incident. This bird is understood to be a medium through which evil spirits give warnings. When it flies in certain directions or sings in a particular way, people believe that spirits are using it to give them a message they must heed. It might be ordering them not to proceed on a journey or continue the work they are doing. To disobey the bird is to risk grave consequences.

Two old men, Flores and Alfredo, told us about an incident with the ichaw bird. Each had laboured for a month clearing relatively small garden plots for their families on the side of a steep hill. Using traditional tools, they had felled trees, pulled out roots and cleared away grass and weeds. It was backbreaking work for those old men.

They slept in makeshift shelters near their gardens rather than hike back and forth over steep mountain trails each day. It was hard being away from their homes, but that was the only land available for gardens.

The two had just finished their work and were about to begin planting vegetable seedlings when an ichaw bird flew over both their garden plots.

Alfredo was fortunate. The bird had flown over his garden from top to bottom, so he could continue working. But when Flores saw the bird, his heart sank and he was gripped with fear. The bird had flown from one side to the other. Although bitterly disappointed, he abandoned his hard-won garden plot. "If I had gone ahead and planted that garden," he said, "someone in my family would have become ill and perhaps even died. Such is the vengeance of the spirits if we ignore their warning."

Fài related a similar story. Just as he was putting the finishing touches to a new veranda on his house, an omen bird flew under it. He immediately stopped his work and began tearing down the new veranda. He would start all over again. He knew that if he ignored the bird, he or a family member would suffer and perhaps die.

The influence of the ichaw bird was wide-ranging. If men were leaving the village to hunt animals for food, they would listen for the call of the ichaw as they went. If they heard what they considered was a happy call, they would continue on their way. But if the call sounded sad, they knew they would offend the spirits by proceeding further, so they would turn back and try again the following day. They might try unsuccessfully several days running, but they knew that only fools dared to disregard the call of the ichaw.

Our response to their beliefs

We could have simply dismissed all we were seeing and hearing as irrational superstition. After all, the so-called "omen" bird was only a bird, wasn't it? But we didn't. We knew it was unwise to dismiss anything as mere fable. Too many bizarre things happened to people to deny the power of the spirit world that was clearly controlling their lives.

There was so much pain and uncertainty in the lives of these people. We were certain that we had the answer to their fear, the Word of God, and we desperately wanted to share it with them. We had a lot to do yet and we still had much to learn. We still had to gain their trust. The waiting would be hard for we would see many more die without faith in Christ, and therefore without hope, before we would see the Word of God in the hands, hearts and minds of these people.

As we came to know the Kalinga people better and began to understand their utter helplessness, even we experienced some of the fear that the Kalingas felt. From time to time we had to remind each other that we were God's children and nothing could touch us beyond what He allowed. God had sent us there, and we knew He would not abandon us there.

Another World

We wanted to understand the Kalinga people, their way of life, and to identify with them in every way possible. That was not an easy task given the constraints of their culture, but it was not our goal to change their culture. Our goal was to give them the life-giving Word of God. As they came to the Lord—and we prayed many would—He would be the one to do any changing that was needed, just as He had done with us when we believed.

We readily acknowledged that our very presence in Mallango would have some influence for change. We brought medicines for treating their illnesses. The alternatives were usually a 50 km trip to the clinic or seeing the sick one die.

We had no farmland, so we bought everything we needed. We also paid wages to people for language and translation help, though we were careful to pay no more than the average salary of a schoolteacher; some teachers were jealous that people who had no formal training were being paid to "teach" us. We used a gas stove for cooking because we owned no trees from which to cut firewood.

We could have bought land and taken time to cultivate it and grow our own vegetables, taken a whole day every week to get firewood from the forest and cooked with wood, one dish at a time. We could have done a lot of things like the local people, but we wouldn't have had much time to do the work we went there to do.

Instead of using a bucket shower, we could have walked to the spring to bathe. That had its own natural constraints. Women had to bathe fully clothed, while men bathed naked but with their backs to passers-by. On one of the few occasions I did bathe at a spring by the trail, I was just reaching for my clothes when an old lady suddenly walked around the corner and found me quite unprepared for company. Seeing me reaching hastily for my pants, she burst out laughing. Years later she was still reminding me and others of the incident.

Sometimes our attempts at being involved in the culture found us more deeply immersed in it than we really cared to be. Once when liquor was stolen from the little village store, the owner called a shaman to perform a ritual that would identify the thief. Every male in the village over twelve years of age was summoned to the store; that included me! My foreignness wasn't sufficient excuse for exemption.

When I arrived, I noticed that a large clay jar, normally used for storing the sweet-tasting sugar cane wine that some brewed, had been placed on the ground. When everyone had assembled, the shaman spoke. "Each of you must drink from this jar," she said. "As you do so, you will swear that you did not steal the liquor." She paused as she looked around the circle of wide-eyed men. "If you are lying, we will know you are the thief, for you will die!"

A murmur of protest came from some of the men. I remained silent. I prayed quietly. A teenager asked his father, "Has this ever been done in Mallango before?" "No, son," he replied, "but I remember hearing about an incident in another village some years ago. As one man, after claiming to be innocent, drank the wine his stomach suddenly swelled and burst. He died a horrible death, and they said it was awful to watch."

Most of the men were skeptical about this process, however, and no one was confident that the guilty person would be discovered. In fact, many feared that an innocent person would be declared guilty. They knew the spirits couldn't be trusted and might want to play a trick on someone who had nothing to do with the theft.

A thought also occurred to me: Wouldn't the spirits have a ball if I was the one declared guilty!

A few of the men tried to slip away quietly but were called back. No one was allowed to leave. A deathly hush fell over the group as our attention focused on the first man in line. He dipped a mug in the jar, swore his innocence and then drank a little wine. He paused for a few seconds, then scurried back to rejoin the anxious onlookers, obviously relieved that for him the ordeal was over. It occurred to me that the guilty person was probably several kilometres away at this moment.

The ritual continued. The next man in the long line reluctantly took his sip of wine. I had never seen the men of Mallango so reluctant to drink their local brew.

Then it was my turn.

I was really nervous as I stepped forward and took the cup from the shaman's hand. Although I knew I was innocent and so did the spirits, I realised I was taking a risk. I thought, What if the spirits decide this is a good time to get rid of me? Nevertheless, I felt I had to go through with it.

I dipped some wine, declared my innocence and drank. As I handed the cup back to the shaman, my hand was shaking. And with a sigh of relief clearly noticed and remarked on light-heartedly by all those near me, I rejoined the watching group. I hoped that the men appreciated my going through this ordeal with them. It was another opportunity to identify with the community, to help them see how much we wanted to be part of it.

No one died that time. Everyone was relieved to walk away unscathed. And no one, except the store owner and the shaman, really cared who the thief was.

Heartache

One night, Saryong told us how his understanding and faith in God had grown. He was telling others about Him, but despite his zeal, he was becoming more and more discouraged. "People are saying you are just bringing another sect here," he told us. "And they are criticising me because of my involvement with you. They say, 'Saryong, you know how many sects have come into Mallango. And every one of them has failed within a year. Those who joined them felt badly let down when they realised how they were deceived.

What makes you think this belief that you are promoting so enthusiastically won't also fail?'"

"I am finding their words very harsh," he added. "Even my relatives are telling me to stop talking about God because they are being criticised too."

Judith and I tried to find words to encourage him, but what did we know about persecution? We had never experienced anything worse than the flippant sarcasm of work mates regarding our faith. Our efforts to encourage Saryong seemed rather weak and unconvincing.

We didn't see Saryong for a few days. The next time we saw him, he was distressed. "I cannot talk about God any more," he said, a look of resignation on his face. "I won't give up my faith," he added, "but because of my stand for the Lord, my family is being ridiculed. I cannot go on letting them suffer because of me."

What could we say? No words came. As we watched him turn and slowly walk away, the realisation that the following day we were going to a workshop at Bagabag and leaving Saryong alone in his anguish left us feeling totally dejected.

Early next morning we reluctantly made our way through the village to the airstrip, trying to think of something helpful to say to Saryong. But he wasn't home, and no one knew where he had gone. Was he deliberately avoiding us? We worried a lot about him during the six weeks we were away.

Gaspar came with us this time to help us work on a grammar write-up, although his wife was pregnant and expected to deliver their first child within a month or so. Gaspar would be back in Mallango in good time. He seemed to enjoy being at Bagabag, but at breakfast on the Wednesday morning of our second week there, he seemed agitated. When I asked him what was wrong, he stammered, "My wife had a son last Sunday!"

We asked how he could know that, as he hadn't heard from his wife or anyone else in Mallango since we had arrived at

Another World

Bagabag. He said, "Last night I had a dream. My grandmother told me about my wife delivering our child. I must return home immediately." Reluctant both to believe that the message in his dream was true and also to let him go at a critical time in our work, I arranged for a flight to take him home.

When he arrived, he was able to send a message back with the pilot: His wife had indeed given birth the previous Sunday, exactly as he had been told in his dream.

FIVE

In the Thick of Things

Beginning Bible Translation

On our return to Mallango, we were greeted by a delighted Udchus. He told us he'd been talking about God and the Bible with lots of people, including some youths from another language group whom he had met in Tabuk, the provincial capital. To our knowledge he hadn't made a profession of faith yet! We realised that God was doing something in him.

By now I felt sufficiently confident in the language to begin translating the Bible. I chose the Gospel of Mark for our first effort. Being mostly narrative, it would be quicker to translate than the other Gospels. I asked Udchus to help me and he nervously agreed to try.

Since the first chapter contains several concepts that we thought would be difficult for a Kalinga to grasp, such as baptism, the kingdom of God, and fishing for people rather than fish, we decided to start with the second chapter. We made excellent progress the first day. I thought ten verses was a reasonable goal, but we translated seventeen.

Judith and I were elated. This was God's Word, and here we were helping to make it available for a group of people who had never before had even a single phrase of the Bible in their language. We felt as if we were on holy ground.

It was all new to Udchus—a crippled man is lowered through a roof by four friends; Jesus forgives the man's sins; someone claims that only God can forgive sins; Jesus calls a man to follow Him as His disciple, and he does! When I asked

77

In the Thick of Things

Udchus at the end of the day what he thought about translation work, he smiled broadly and said, "Awad kanasna! (It's fun!)"

"Would you like to do some more tomorrow?" I asked.

"Yes!" he replied eagerly.

His eagerness was to be short-lived.

Udchus enjoyed his work immensely the first week, but on the Monday of the second week he didn't come. We guessed he was sick. At noon I went to his house to see him, but he wasn't there and no one knew where he was.

Early that afternoon I happened to glance out the window and saw him walking towards our house. I called out eagerly, "Hey, 'Chus! It's good you're coming to work."

"I'm sorry," he replied, "I won't be working with you today. I don't know when I will be able to help you again." And without a word of explanation he walked away.

Two days later he came back to work on the translation with no attempt to explain his absence. But his appearances over the next few days were sporadic and his enthusiasm seemed to have vanished. Confused, I asked Juanito, a neighbour of Udchus, if he knew what was going on. His reply was cutting: "He's your friend and you don't know? Udchus is being ridiculed in the village for helping you."

We tried talking with Udchus about it but couldn't find sufficient words to help him or us. He suggested we look for someone else to work for a few weeks to allow him time to think about his future commitment. But we knew we wouldn't find anyone else willing to help full-time. And even if we did convince another of our friends to help, they would also suffer ridicule.

That night with us both feeling totally dejected, Judith summed up our feelings. She said, "It'll be a miracle if we get this New Testament finished."

We started reading 1 Corinthians 15 together and suddenly verse 58 seemed to jump right off the page and grab both of us: "...be strong and steady, always enthusiastic about the Lord's work, for you know that nothing you do for the Lord is ever useless" (NLT).

It was just what we needed. We knew we could keep going.

Next morning we'd just finished breakfast when Udchus appeared at the door. He had come back to work. Within six weeks we completed the first draft of Mark's Gospel.

There was still a lot to do—checking, revising, more checking—but completing the first draft of Mark was cause for great celebration. The first book of the Bible in the language of the Southern Kalinga people would soon be printed and available to them. Udchus was as happy and relieved to reach this point as Judith and I were.

Just one week later our joy faded yet again.

Our world falls apart

One morning after breakfast I felt compelled to go and visit Saryong. Coffee was brewing and he offered me some. As we sat drinking, he told me that Iminya, a young woman living at the other end of the village, was controlled by a spirit. He suggested I go to see her.

My initial response was to return home. I had no desire at all to get involved. This was an area outside my experience, and I preferred to keep it that way. But as I reflected on what Jesus would have done in a situation like this, I decided to go and find out what was happening.

Nervously, I made my way towards Iminya's house and found many of the village men sitting on the ground drinking wine and talking together animatedly. Others were preparing to kill a water buffalo. Inside I found the house packed with women and children.

Iminya was seated on the floor. Her husband, Falliyaw, sat behind her, holding her tightly. She looked tired and frightened, her face was drawn and her frail body was shaking uncontrollably. During the odd moments when she was coherent, women plied her with questions.

"Why has this happened to you?" they asked. "Which spirit have you offended?" But there was no response.

For two hours I watched, praying for guidance. Should I try to help her? What would happen if I did? What would the people think if I got involved? Anyway, I'd had no experience in this sort of thing. I was scared. But I thought, "What would Jesus do?" Finally, my mind spinning from all my conflicting thoughts, I asked Emilio, Iminya's brother-in-law, if I could try to cast the spirit out of her.

"Of course!" he said. "You can't do any harm." So I moved closer to Iminya, with no idea what I would do next.

After an urgent prayer for God's protection, I said in shaky Kalinga, "You spirit! In the Name of Jesus Christ I drive you out! You should not be in this woman. Jesus Christ is stronger than you. Leave her now!"

A strange voice came from Iminya's lips. It wasn't Iminya's normal voice. "You're Bruce," it said. "You're a rich man. You have your own aeroplane."

"It's trying to change the subject," Emilio whispered. "It wants to deceive the people, to make them jealous of you so they won't want you to continue what you're doing here."

"If I am to leave this woman," the voice continued, "a water buffalo must be killed as payment." I tried several more times to convince the spirit to leave, but without success. Instead it kept repeating its demand.

I stayed with Iminya for another hour and talked to the spirit several more times, but it refused to leave her. Then someone said, "Ask for its name. If it tells its name, its power will be weakened." I tried doing that, and others joined in too, but instead of revealing its own name it repeated over and over, "You're Bruce. You're a rich man. You have your own aeroplane."

In the Thick of Things

Finally the spirit agreed to reveal its name, but only
through the shaman. Ampug was summoned and she began to
converse with the spirit. This time it spoke through Ampug's
mouth, but it still refused to state its name. Instead, it repeated
its demand that a water buffalo be slaughtered.

After much persistence, the spirit suddenly revealed where
it came from. I don't remember the place it named, but I do
recall everyone was surprised at the admission. "We're getting
somewhere now," said one of the men. "We'll soon know its
name." It spoke several times during the next hour, but each
time it named a different place as its origin and no one present
knew which, if indeed any, was correct.

Iminya's husband decided he could wait no longer and
ordered their water buffalo killed. At that moment Iminya
convulsed. Everyone in the house began screaming and
wailing, their eyes staring wildly in fear. I felt anxious.
I didn't know whether to stay or leave.

The commotion continued for about ten minutes. Then
I heard shouting outside, the bellowing of the water buffalo,
and then a thud as a machete split its skull. An eerie silence
suddenly took over. The spirit's demands had been met.

Within minutes, however, it was evident that the spirit
had not left Iminya after all. She began shaking uncontrollably
again. Someone cried out in frustration, "What else do you
want?" There was no reply.

After a while I left the house thoroughly exhausted.

Next morning, Saryong reported that Iminya's condition
was unchanged. During the night she had been shaking and
yelling. Nine men were needed to restrain her when it
appeared she might injure herself. The spirit had demanded
a pig as an offering that morning.

Neither Judith nor I felt strong enough to see her. In fact,
we tried to put her out of our minds and instead concentrate
on translation, but we simply couldn't. What was our responsibility as Christians to this poor woman? We were the only ones

81

with the real answer to her dilemma. But we didn't know how to go about helping her.

Two days later I typed out three passages from Mark's Gospel in which Jesus dealt with spirits. Then with considerable apprehension, I walked to Iminya's house. Judith prayed during the hour I was away.

When I arrived only Iminya's husband, Falliyaw, and a few women were with her. I talked with Falliyaw first, and he asked Iminya if she knew who I was. "I know you," she said weakly, "you are Bruce." Before she could say more, I interrupted and nervously asked her to listen while I read some words of God.

She listened in silence. As I read, Falliyaw and others repeated some phrases, and when I finished everyone wanted to discuss what they had heard. After a few minutes, I said, "Iminya, I want to pray for you again." I could hardly believe what I was saying!

As I prayed, a strange feeling came over me. It was as though I were no longer in control—as if it were Someone else speaking while I was just listening. Iminya repeated some of my words while I was praying, and even asked me questions. She seemed quite coherent. When I finished I said, "If you believe God can remove this spirit, and you really want Him to, He will." She said nothing.

Next morning a sense of great relief could be felt all over the village. Someone said to us, "There's good news! The spirit left Iminya during the night. It's because you read to her from the Bible!"

But that night the spirit returned.

I visited Iminya again the following morning and found she wasn't as agitated this time. When the spirit demanded another sacrifice, I was amazed to hear Iminya and some of her relatives cursing it and refusing to comply with its demands. Some were even encouraging her to trust God.

The attention of the whole village was focused on Iminya that day. When one woman entered the house, Iminya spoke to her in Ilocano, a language she had never learnt to speak. And when a woman from another village came to visit her, Iminya told everyone present the secret sins of that woman, to her extreme embarrassment. People realised it was the spirit that was speaking. The hardest thing for Iminya's family, however, was that she didn't recognise her own children.

Later that day the spirit gave its name—that of Iminya's mother who had died 30 years before. She had also been controlled by a spirit at one time. Iminya began to improve after that, and within hours she appeared to be in her right mind again.

I was exhausted by the whole experience, and during the next few days felt weaker and weaker. On the fourth morning I could hardly move. A headache developed, and that evening I had a high fever and my whole body shook uncontrollably for nearly two hours. Thinking it was malaria, I took anti-malarial tablets twice during the night, but vomited them up. The pain in my head became excruciating.

By dawn I felt even worse so I said to Judith, "You'd better get on the radio and ask for a flight to Bagabag. I need to get away from here for a while." Judith and the children had to do all the packing up; I was too weak to help them. When the pilot called to tell us he was on his way, we left the house. I staggered as if drunk through the village, using two sticks for support.

Someone laughed, and called out, "You're a pitiful sight, Bruce!" Another joked, "You should let us carry you in a blanket!" I laughed. "I can manage by myself," I lied. I could imagine them years later, still laughing if I had agreed to their suggestion. "How pitiful Bruce looked when he was carried to the airstrip," they would have said. And, "Didn't he look comical, slung from a pole in a blanket! And wasn't he heavy! It took six men to manage the load!"

As I staggered past Iminya's house, I asked Emilio to tell her that she really needed to trust Jesus and invite Him into her life. Otherwise the spirit might return and bring others with it. Just as Jesus warned in Matthew 12, when an evil spirit comes out of a person, if it doesn't find anywhere suitable to go it will return to the "house" (meaning the person) that it left. If it finds the house unoccupied, it will re-enter and bring with it seven other spirits more evil than itself to live there, leaving the person worse off than before. Iminya should ask Jesus in, as it were, so that when the spirit returned it would find the house, Iminya, occupied and would leave her alone. I didn't hear her response. I was too occupied trying to stay on my feet.

The plane was a welcome sight. So was Bagabag. I spent the next two weeks on my back, my head constantly pounding and feeling nauseous the whole time. I couldn't eat and lost several kilos.

Around noon on our fifteenth day at Bagabag, as I lay on my back wondering about my illness and what had caused it, Iminya's face suddenly appeared in my mind. I thought, Is it possible my illness could have something to do with her? Could a spirit be bothering me?

I rejected the idea. Spirits couldn't affect a child of God like this! But after a while I began to wonder if they could. If spirits were somehow affecting me, what should I do? Should I confront them? I prayed for the Lord's protection. Rather timidly and with a soft voice I said, "If there are any spirits bothering me, I command you to leave me alone."

I felt no different. After praying for several minutes, my confidence increased. Then I said loudly, "In the Name of Jesus, get away from me, you spirits!"

Within seconds I began to feel better! My head stopped hurting. The nausea decreased remarkably. I didn't understand what was happening, but I sensed something supernatural was going on. Two days later I felt normal, so we decided to return to Mallango. We were delighted to be able to arrange a flight for the following morning.

Arriving at the Mallango airstrip, we were puzzled that no one came to meet us. Usually at least twenty children and a dozen adults would be at the strip by the time we landed. As soon as the plane could be heard approaching, they would come running, looking like a wave on a distant beach as they raced towards the strip. But for the first time there was no one running. In fact, we could see no movement at all, and there was a strange, eerie feeling about the place.

Then the pilot left us. As we watched the plane disappear over the next mountain, we suddenly felt very much alone. The walk through the village to our house at the far end only intensified our uneasiness, for apart from the village children no one seemed happy to see us. No one joked with us like they normally did, laughing about the "vacation" we had just had. Every time we left the village, for whatever reason, the people would call it a "vacation."

Those who did respond to our greetings seemed half-hearted about it and reluctant to converse further with us. We were completely perplexed by what appeared to us as rejection.

"Has someone died?" we asked a teenager. That could explain the silence and the lack of enthusiasm. "No," he replied. So what was going on? Our children hadn't noticed anything wrong. They were soon off playing with their young friends who seemed quite happy to see them. But why were the adults ignoring us? We concluded that it must have been our imagination; we were expecting too much wanting them to welcome us enthusiastically every time we arrived—until we heard about Iminya.

One of her relatives finally agreed to tell us what had happened. Spirits had taken control of Iminya—a large number of spirits—and she was in deep trouble, far worse than at any time previously.

She had been fine most of the time we were away, and had even been to work in her fields. But without any warning, spirits had entered her again. She had become so violent that a cage had to be built inside the house to restrain her, and her children were afraid to go near her.

Judith said, "When we left here three weeks ago, she seemed quite normal. When did the spirits return?"

"Three days ago, at noon."

We froze. That was the exact moment I had begun to recover. I felt weak; a wave of nausea swept through me. Then a stinging rebuke was aimed at me: "If you had not interfered and read those words of God, this would not have happened!"

A few days later the spirits declared that they would stop tormenting Iminya if she would agree to become a shaman. To indicate her acceptance of their offer, she was to place a bowl with a white cloth over it in the rafters of her house.

At first she refused, though she knew of other women who had complied with such an order and had been immediately healed. But Iminya didn't want to be a shaman. She was still in her early thirties. Some older people, however, urged her to obey. "You won't have to serve as a shaman until you are much older," they tried to assure her. When she agreed to consider the offer, a remarkable change came over her. She became calm and was soon allowed to leave her cage.

But the spirits continued to control her. Later that week as she walked to the spring with her water container resting on a cloth on her head, she heard a voice. "I see you are almost ready to obey us!" She looked around but there was no one there. Then she realised that the cloth on her head was white, and of course it was above her.

A week later, Iminya's family butchered a pig to indicate to the spirits that they, at least, were willing to let her become a shaman, even if she wasn't yet willing. Next day they killed a hen in an attempt to seal the deal. They all knew the spirits would still possess her, but would stop tormenting her once she was "ordained." If she continued to refuse their demands, the spirits threatened to make her blind or drown her.

Iminya still resisted her family's pleas and refused to give in. A few nights later she became violent again. Her family, feeling anger but also complete helplessness, reluctantly put her back in the cage.

Next day a shaman came from another village, claiming he could heal Iminya. He told her that Satan had given him a special gift of healing, and that he could cast out the spirits in her by calling on his own spirit-companion who was stronger than all the spirits in her. He did this, then gave her some herbs and advised her to leave her home and live somewhere else.

Iminya and her family moved to her parents' home. Once again she seemed normal for a while. But three weeks later the violent, erratic behaviour returned. She seemed worse than ever, and her children ran away from her in terror as she approached them.

Her husband realised the spirits had returned yet again, and there was no alternative—she had to be put back in the cage again. This time her arms were tied with telephone wire. Twice during the night she escaped from the cage, breaking her bonds with superhuman strength.

When morning came, Iminya decided she could fight the spirits no longer. To the relief of her family, she took a bowl and a white cloth and placed them high up in the rafters of her home.

She was not troubled from that moment on. The attitude of the people towards us rapidly improved. We were relieved at least about that because progress on translation had taken a battering during this saga.

Heartbreak

After a long break, Saryong came back to work with us on translation. We were happy to employ both him and Udchus since they worked only part-time. But something was still wrong. Saryong wasn't himself. He was obviously under some sort of strain that he wouldn't talk about.

In the Thick of Things

One day he told us how he had been so hurt by people's comments to him that for the previous three months he had not talked to anyone about the Lord. That was hurting him even more than the comments. He wanted others to know God's Good News, but no one seemed interested.

One of the main reasons for the bitterness of village people towards Saryong was his refusal to follow Kalinga customs regarding the spirits. Another was that he received wages from us for his language and translation work. Although we paid him only a modest wage—about the same as a school-teacher—many insisted that since Saryong had not finished his college degree he did not deserve to be treated as if he had. "What they really want is that I won't be successful at any-thing," he told us, "especially working for you."

Although we should have been prepared for his next com-ment, it still took us by surprise and came as a devastating blow. "My dear friends," he said, his head bowed. "I'm sorry, but I can't work for you any longer. I can't handle the people's criticism any more."

He turned and walked out. Our hearts sank yet again.

However, a few days later something happened that changed Saryong's mind and renewed our rapidly waning enthusiasm to continue the work. It began with the sickness of Tiw-an, the leader of the Espiritistas (Spiritualists) in Mallango, a sect that had been very influential in the lives of perhaps 30 people for about a year. Sickness was not part of their doctrine, so when Tiw-an became ill the leader of the Espiritistas in Tabuk, the provincial capital, was summoned. After examining Tiw-an, he declared, "This is just a test. On the fifteenth day of his illness, he will recover."

But on the fourteenth day of his illness he died.

During those two weeks, Tiw-an had been able to move only his eyes and one hand. He ate nothing and drank little. His wife and children had refused to take him to the hospital, fearing they would all die if they did. Such was the hold that the sect had over them.

On the fifteenth day, the day after he died, I decided to visit his family. I felt nervous as I approached their home. A bizarre thought occurred to me: Maybe I'd find Tiw-an alive again, raised from the dead! But when I saw his wasted corpse, just skin and bone, I knew that a return to life for him wasn't on anyone's cards!

From that day on, for some reason we couldn't work out, the people's attitude towards Saryong seemed to change. No one actually explained why that was so, but it was obvious there was a new respect for him.

Saryong had been convinced no one else would ever believe in Christ, but now he began to have confidence that some would. His newly regained enthusiasm was so contagious that we caught it too. We would continue our work in Mallango—again.

"There must be some way," Saryong said, "to make the Gospel clear to my people—some way they will understand it and accept it."

One evening he asked me to bring the first few chapters of the draft of Mark's Gospel to his house. He had tapes of gospel songs in the Balangao language. He began to play them loudly, hoping to arouse the curiosity of his neighbours enough to make them come in and hear the Scripture he wanted to read to them. Three men came inside to see what was going on.

After offering them coffee, Saryong read the first chapter of Mark aloud and asked them how they might improve the translation. All three were happy to offer suggestions.

After they left, Saryong said to me, "This might be a good way to start a Bible study. Getting people to help us straighten the words will get the words into their minds!" I was willing to try anything that would both encourage him and expose people to the Word of God.

In the Thick of Things

Next night we tried the same method of attracting an audience, but it was raining heavily and no one came. The following night was clear, but still no one came. It looked as if Saryong's plan wasn't going to work the way we had hoped. But he wasn't so easily discouraged now. He simply said, "That's okay. We will think of another way." It was a wonderful relief to see his enthusiasm back.

Next morning he said, "I'll select some men to check Mark with us, and we will pay them. If there's money in it, we will get all the help we need." When we discussed the way we would tackle the work with the men, Saryong said, "We'll start with sections that have plenty of action. That will capture their attention. I'll arrange it. You come here tomorrow afternoon and we'll begin."

Judith and I prayed for Saryong and the men who might come. We desperately wanted this idea to work, mainly for Saryong's sake.

Straight after lunch next day, I walked quickly to Saryong's house, excited about his latest plan. Six men were with him. I didn't recognise any of them but that was okay. They must have come from another village but I didn't mind who he got to help. It was going to work!

My excitement rapidly diminished when Saryong told me they were not the ones he had invited, but were just visiting. "Perhaps they would be willing to look at Mark," I suggested quickly, wanting to seize on this interruption as an opportunity to introduce the translation to other villages. "I'm sorry," he simply replied, "but our plan will have to be changed."

I was disappointed, and from the expression on Saryong's face I could tell he was too. I sat and talked with them for a couple of hours, then returned home.

A week passed. Saryong's plan had still not progressed any further. Judith and I were again beginning to feel despondent about the future of our work in Mallango. It didn't take much to get us feeling that way.

Then we overheard Saryong explaining his faith to a group of women outside our house. Later he again shared with us his deep concern for the spiritual welfare of his people and his longing for others to also believe. Our despondency evaporated.

However, that evening while we were visiting Saryong, some of his neighbours started talking loudly outside, no doubt so that he could hear every word they said. "He thinks he's important, working for the foreigners," one sneered. "Perhaps he thinks he's better than us with his religious talk and working with books."

Although we knew it hurt him to hear people talking so vindictively, we were overjoyed when he turned to us and said with a look of great determination, "I must continue because it's the Word of God, and it's the most important work anyone could do."

We were encouraged again! Saryong's involvement was vital. We would need help from others too if we were to do all the checking of the translation that was required. No one was volunteering, however, so we prayed. The answer to our prayers seemed to come with a group of men that I approached one evening. They agreed to help so I asked Saryong to come and join us next morning.

Soon after breakfast I walked to the home of one of them. Inside eight men were waiting to help us check Mark's Gospel. Saryong arrived a little late, curious about what was happening. As he looked around at the men, I could tell he was uneasy about something. Taking me aside he whispered, "This won't work! These men are the village 'philosophisers'—that's what we call people whose favourite entertainment is destroying with words. I have no doubt that they want to spoil our work. They will pretend to correct the translation, and their explanations will be so convincing that you will believe them. But they will really be tricking you rather than helping you."

In the Thick of Things

I was confused. It seemed just a little too bizarre to believe. Surely they wouldn't do that to me. I was so desperate for help that I was prepared to take a risk with them. "I'll be ready," I told Saryong. "At the first sign of trouble I'll deal with it."

Before we started I explained the importance of accurate, idiomatic translation, and how much I would value their help in revising our work where it needed improvement. Early in the day I felt on two occasions that their suggestions were not good, and wondered if they might be mistaken. I was quick to comment the first time. Before I could comment the second time, one of them did it for me. I decided they were either genuinely wrong in their suggestions or they were just joking with me. I didn't believe they were making deliberate mistakes.

We worked for ten hours that day, and all the changes that were suggested made sense to me. It seemed a very profitable time. Saryong seemed quite relaxed, and he explained several passages to them as the day went on, hoping they would learn something and gain a respect for God and His Word.

That night Saryong and I debriefed on the day's activity. He agreed with me that it had been worthwhile. On the second morning only five came, but I was confident they would do what we wanted just as they had the first day.

It started out even better than the first day. During the first hour they found dozens of ways to improve the translation, and all of them made sense to me. It was obvious that they understood exactly what I wanted, and the more excited I became the more willing they were to help. I realised after a little while, however, that Saryong hadn't said much. He was quiet most of the time, offering just an occasional opinion. But that was okay, I thought. He might not want to discuss everything right there but instead look at any minor problems with me later.

I was more than a little disappointed that my work needed such massive revision, but I was grateful that we were finding the problems now rather than later after it was printed.

By mid-morning Saryong had dropped right out of the discussion. He seemed agitated and became more and more fidgety as the morning passed. He even looked angry at times. I couldn't understand why he was acting that way, but decided to wait and talk to him at our lunch break. I continued to take careful notes of all the suggested changes, enthusiastically expressing my gratitude again and again to the men for their help.

After they left us for lunch, I said to Saryong, "Wasn't that wonderful? They were so helpful...."

Saryong cut me off. "You don't understand," he said, trembling. "You thought they were helping you, but since the first hour, every suggestion they've given you was wrong. I knew what they were doing, but I couldn't say anything. They were deliberately trying to destroy our work! Can't you see they hate us?"

"No!" I gasped. "That's impossible! You must be mistaken. No one could be that vindictive."

Could I have been so foolish? As I thought back over the morning, and looked again at my notes, it slowly began to sink in that Saryong was right. I was devastated. I tried apologising to Saryong but he was in no mood to listen. So I picked up my notes, shuffled out the door, and went home.

As I began to tell Judith what had happened, I burst into tears. Judith watched helplessly as I sat there weeping for half an hour. When I was able to speak, I sobbed out the account of my naivety.

I cancelled the afternoon session and went to lie down. Neither of us felt like doing anything. We tried talking to God about it. Our children sensed something was wrong and asked us what it was, but we just said we felt sick. We did! Saryong didn't come to help us again for several weeks.

In the Thick of Things

Revenge

One morning the village was abnormally quiet. I hadn't been out for my usual coffee run and no one had called to find out why. Not one person had walked past our house while we were eating breakfast. There wasn't even the usual hubbub of children playing games. Curious, Judith and I decided to go for a walk.

There was no one to be seen anywhere. It felt strange, as if the village was deserted. Seeing a neighbour through a partially open door, we called out, "*Furun* (friend), where is everybody?"

"In their houses," came the muffled reply. "Kamakam hit William last night and now his relatives want revenge."

He told us that during the night, a young fellow named Kamakam had got drunk and attacked William, knocking him unconscious with a piece of wood. William had been taken to the hospital 50 km away. Fortunately he wasn't dead, but since in Kalinga culture striking is equivalent to killing, the people were treating the incident like a murder.

Kamakam and his brother—his closest relative—were in hiding because they expected that someone from William's family would try to kill one of them. If they couldn't be located, some other close relative would probably be the victim of their vengeance. All the members of Kamakam's family, including his first cousins, were being guarded by more distant relatives. Since everyone in Mallango was related in some way to everyone else, no one felt safe.

A solution, however, was possible. If William and his family would agree to accept a rice field and a water buffalo from Kamakam, that would settle the matter for now. That would still not guarantee, however, that the matter would end entirely. Decades later, William's grandson, or even his great-grandson, might decide that the payment wasn't enough and take revenge by killing a descendent of Kamakam. Kalingas have long memories, but for the moment the family would be safe.

94

At any future time, if William or a relative was to injure or kill anyone on Kamakam's side, William would have to butcher something to feed all the relatives on both sides. If he didn't, the stomachs of all those related to William would swell and burst. If they purposely took revenge later, there would be no end to revenge killing between the families.

If a machete had been used rather than a stick, the settlement would have been much greater. A few years ago, Lamfayung from Bangad attacked a fellow with a machete, cutting his hand off and wounding him on the head. As payment, Lamfayung and all his brothers, sisters and first cousins had to each give a field to the family of the wounded man, and Lamfayung lost everything. He also had to contract his children in marriage to children of the wounded man.

The *opas* ritual

William returned from the hospital bruised and sore but otherwise well. He and his relatives still had to agree on the terms of settlement, but before proceeding any further, they wanted to do the opas ceremony.

The shaman who specialises in conducting the opas ceremony is usually a woman. During the ritual, she puts an unfortunate hen in a sack and waves it around her head. Then holding a bowl covered with a white cloth, she recites an incantation to call up certain spirits.

Normally she expects to see two spirits, one with horns and long teeth, the other the spirit of the victim who is still alive. A ball of the victim's hair then appears floating in the air, landing either on the cloth she is holding or on a blanket spread on the ground. Just like all the other rituals in traditional Kalinga culture, no one questioned its authenticity.

Some years before, Allit was on a bus that drove over an embankment and tumbled down a ravine. "I survived the experience," Allit said, "but I felt unwell for several weeks and my body continually seemed heavy. So I called the shaman to perform the opas ritual for me. Before the ritual could begin, I had to butcher a pig. The shaman had me sit on the floor and she covered me with a blanket. Then she took a gong and held it so that it would catch any hairs that would appear and drop—from somewhere. During the ritual hairs from all the other passengers on the bus appeared and fell into the gong. At that moment I felt fine and my body was no longer heavy."

Saryong told us of an incident involving his father some 40 years previously. "After my father's fall down a cliff," he said, "our family had the opas performed. During the ritual a ball of hair appeared and floated around the room, then it fell onto a new blanket spread on the floor. There were about 1,000 hairs in the ball, all the same colour as my father's hair. We believed that to be a good omen. My father would make a good recovery from his injuries—and he did."

If something similar occurred in William's opas, it would mean he would also recover—though to us he seemed quite healthy already.

When the shaman announced that the most auspicious day for the ceremony had arrived, I decided to join the group gathered in William's house. About twenty other men were there. There was complete silence from the onlookers as the shaman began her incantation.

Several minutes passed and not one hair appeared. I asked Chagchakan what the shaman would do if the ritual failed. He replied, "If no hairs appear, that will signify there is an unbeliever present who is preventing its success. The shaman will see a spirit with the face of the offender, and then she will look at everyone present to see whose face matches it. That person will be expected to butcher a pig. If he doesn't, something serious will happen to him. He might even die."

I began to feel a steadily growing uneasiness as the minutes passed and still no hairs appeared. I even found myself hoping to see some!

After waiting more than ten minutes, the shaman began to look around those gathered for a particular face—the face of the "unbeliever." All eyes in the room followed her search.

Since I fully expected the offending face to be mine, I decided it was time to exit—quickly—but my legs wouldn't respond. Then just as my stomach began tying itself into knots, the shaman's head suddenly stopped moving. She picked two hairs up off the floor and instantly deemed the ceremony a success. That outcome seemed quite unusual to many of those watching, but I didn't wait to join the discussion that followed. Instead I slipped quickly and quietly out of the house, vowing never to attend another such ritual if I could help it.

The two families met together later and agreed that Kamakam should give a rice field and a water buffalo to William and also butcher a water buffalo to feed the village. Also Kamakam's first cousin would marry William since intermarriage was the surest way of satisfying all the parties in such a conflict and of preventing further revenge. The last we heard everything happened as planned and all parties were satisfied.

Revenge—and us

Revenge is extremely important to Kalingas. While playing with some village children one day, Elena bumped heads with Elizabeth, who was soon sporting the biggest black eye we'd ever seen. Later Elena's parents brought her to our place and told us that Elizabeth should hit Elena and hurt her as revenge for what she had done to Elizabeth.

We decided we couldn't allow that, and Elizabeth didn't want to hurt her friend either. I guess we were going against the culture, but that's the way it had to be for us in this instance. As it turned out, they appreciated our care.

In the Thick of Things

Making peace

One of the most important aspects of traditional Kalinga life is the *pochon*, or peace pact, a treaty designed to achieve and maintain peace between villages.

This is how Saryong recalled the beginnings of the peace pact.

Long ago the people in the mountains began fighting each other. For a long time the inhabitants of each village couldn't go to their fields or to other villages because they were afraid they'd be ambushed and killed. Everyone just stayed in their own villages. For daily living they had to make do with what they had since they couldn't leave their villages. That situation lasted for several years, but with the lack of variety in their food and the continuous danger they felt, people began to wonder what they could do to relieve their pitiful situation.

Some brave men from one village ventured to another village in a desperate attempt to try trading for what they needed. None of them returned home; the people of the visited village killed them all. That scenario was repeated many times. However, because of their need for food, they were forced to go and find what they could in other places. Every time they tried, though, some were killed and the survivors would return empty-handed to their homes.

Because that kept happening, the leaders in each village started thinking seriously about a solution to their dilemma. One particularly brave, confident man, set out by himself to go to another village to trade. On the way he met some people from that village but he wasn't afraid.

He said to them, "Don't kill me! Instead let's talk together and try to work out what we can do that will benefit each other. Let's be friends instead of enemies. We all have a common need. Through our friendship we'll be able to go to each other's village and exchange what we have for what we need. As a sign of our friendship I will give one of you a machete.

The one who gets my machete will give me a machete
or a spear."

He took out his machete, handed it to one of the men,
and said, "When you return to your village, let everyone there
know about our friendship, and when I return to my village
I'll do the same. The main benefit of the pact that we are
making is that we will no longer kill each other. Any time you
come to our village we'll show hospitality to you, and when we
come to your village you'll show hospitality to us too." Then he
turned and set off for his home.

When he arrived he told his surprised greeters about his
meeting with men from the other village and how he had
forged a pact with them that made it possible for people from
either village to go to the other in safety. Everyone was pleased
to hear what he had done, and from that time on the fighting
and killing between those two villages stopped.

Because their pact worked so successfully, people in one
of the villages said, "Let's multiply our pact. Let's go to other
villages and make peace pacts with them too." That's what
they did; a large group set off on a peace-making journey.

People in faroff areas in the mountains hadn't heard about
the first peace pact. They were still fighting and killing each
other. However, they decided to listen to the men who so
bravely entered their territory, to find out their purpose in
coming. They liked what they heard, and decided to make
a peace pact with them too. Then everyone wanted to be
involved in following it through.

Each village chose a man who was well-off and kind but
also known to be brave. He would be the peace pact holder,
the one who would make sure his village kept their side of the
pact. After each village selected their peace pact holder, five or
ten brave men went with him to yet another village to make a
peace pact with that village.

When they arrived the village people gathered together and
butchered a pig for the visiting peace pact holder. They also

In the Thick of Things

butchered a pig for the visiting peace pact holder. They also drank a jar of wine. The pig they ate and the wine they drank were a seal on the pact being forged. Then they discussed the details of the pact and made laws that would work for the benefit of everyone and be easily understood even by the simplest person.

A peace pact binds two villages together. The word *pochon* literally means "to tie" or "to bind." If an enemy attacks either village, the two villages will join forces and fight the offenders.

Two highly respected men are chosen—one from each village—and appointed as the peace pact holders. If someone breaks the peace pact, it's a very serious matter because it affects the whole community. Both peace pact holders will work together to bring to justice those responsible for breaking the pact.

If someone wounds another from the village with whom his village has a peace pact, the holder of the peace pact in the village of the attacker is permitted to wound him, without further revenge from the offender's family. If the one attacked dies, they are free to kill the attacker.

If someone steals a water buffalo from the other village, he must give three water buffaloes to replace the one he stole, one to the peace pact holder in his own village and two to the man from whom he stole.

Other aspects included telling people about the peace pact wherever they went so that more would hear about it, with the aim of forging peace pacts with other villages too. Marriage is also encouraged between the two villages.

The celebration of a renewed peace pact, with its dancing and singing that went on for several days and nights, was one of the aspects of Kalinga life that we enjoyed the most.

In the incident we heard about when we first arrived at Mallango, several people from Mallango had been planting rice near the road when suddenly what sounded like a volley of gunshots was heard nearby. The people planting thought the sound was from road workers exploding dynamite to clear rocks from the roadside, but shortly afterwards they heard someone shouting. The voice called, "We've been shot by Tulgao people!" The Mallango hearers ran towards the sound of the voice and came across two men from Butbut sprawled on the road. One was unhurt but the other was bleeding freely from one leg. Leaving them, the Mallango men ran further along the road and found three more men. They had all been shot. One was dead, shot in the head. The other two were still alive.

The Mallango men picked up all the wounded and dead and carried them along the road to the next town, Fangad. Then Fangad men carried them to Tinglayan and people from there carried them up to Butbut. Then men from Butbut set off to avenge the killing and wounding of their people.

Since Butbut had a peace pact with Mallango, guaranteeing protection of each village's citizens when in the other's territory, Mallango was technically responsible for the Butbut men's well-being. Tulgao had therefore brought Mallango into disrepute through that incident, and it was fined by Mallango. But that didn't solve the problem between Butbut and Tulgao. Revenge killings continued back and forth for many years afterwards.

SIX

Quitting Time

The Balangaos' first visit

I n October 1976 we asked Joanne Shetler if she thought some of the Balangao elders might like to visit Mallango. We hoped they might encourage Saryong and foster some interest in the Gospel. Jo talked to them.

Their initial response was negative; they couldn't spare the time. After they prayed about it, three of the men sensed that God was telling them to go. They even decided to pay their own travelling expenses and treat it as a missionary outreach from the Balangao church. Along with Jo, the three arrived at Mallango early one morning just two weeks later. The first two men who climbed down out of the plane were Masa-aw and Henry. The third man was Canao.

As Canao climbed out of the plane, we suddenly remembered a scene over three years before when Canao had told us outside Jo Shetler's home in Balangao that he would pray God would send us to the Southern Kalingas. We had put it completely out of our minds at the time since we were planning to head south. However, seeing Canao arrive, we suddenly realised that there was something very significant about where we were: of the more than 100 language groups in the Philippines, we were in Southern Kalinga. God had answered Canao's prayer!

It's hard to describe how we felt just then. Canao wasn't surprised to see us there. He knew God would answer his prayer.

Quitting Time

The realisation that God had answered Canao's prayer helped keep us in Mallango many times during the next few years when things were difficult for us and it would have been much easier to quit and go home.

During the day the Balangaos found it hard to interest anyone in a conversation about the Lord. They persisted, however, and that evening a large number gathered. Over and over again they were asked about creation, sin, and why Satan was banished from heaven. They patiently answered all questions. Later as others joined them, the same questions were asked. Around midnight someone said, "That's enough, friends. You'll be weary from answering the same questions." But Canao replied, "Never mind. I'm happy for you to keep asking until you are satisfied with the answers."

At 2 a.m. everyone finally left them to sleep. They started talking with people again at dawn and continued until 2 a.m. the next morning. Canao later commented to us, "They're very interested. They wouldn't have asked so many questions if they hadn't wanted to know so much."

As they were leaving for home, some of the old men urged them to come back another time. "We want to hear more about Jesus Christ." Saryong added, "It's good that you came to teach the Good News to the people. I have been trying by myself, but it is too hard for me."

I asked Palongpong if he was tired since he had been with the Balangaos most of the time. He replied, "When I'm attending other village gatherings which sometimes last several days, I always get very tired. But they were talking about Jesus Christ and I didn't feel tired at all."

Soon afterwards Saryong came back to work on the translation. We worked well together until mid-December when we left for a couple of weeks' holiday at Bagabag over Christmas. As we boarded the plane, Saryong's last words had been, "Please pray for me and my family—and for the whole of Mallango—every day." We promised we would.

We planned to stay at Bagabag for the translation checking workshop beginning in February where we would have Mark's Gospel checked and prepared for publication. Since Saryong didn't want to leave his family for a whole month, we asked Udchus if he would come and help us. He agreed to come.

Just like rice ready to harvest

Udchus arrived in time for the workshop. He could tell from our enthusiastic welcome that we were relieved to see him. He settled in quickly and seemed happy to be with us. Each day we spent several hours with a colleague who checked the accuracy of our translation using an English translation of the Kalinga text. Each evening Udchus wanted to discuss the verses we had checked that day.

Before breakfast Udchus went to a Bible study with men from the other language groups represented at the workshop. He asked many questions. The others thought he was trying to intimidate them with his many questions, but he insisted he genuinely wanted to learn; he wanted to know how to answer those who would try to intimidate him back in the village, should he believe and then become a teacher of the Good News.

They knew he wasn't a believer yet, and their patience with him made an impression. Even though he felt that his manner of questioning could have made them angry, they remained calm and obviously considerate of him and his need. He decided he wanted to be like them.

Rudy Barlaan, a Filipino colleague, also noticed Udchus' keen interest in the Scriptures and sensed he was close to believing. One day when Udchus was working alone in my office, Rudy came in and sat on his desk. Udchus wondered what he wanted. He began to talk to Udchus about the kingdom of God. After about two hours, he looked at Udchus and asked him, "Would you like to receive Jesus so that He can help you?"

Udchus replied, "Yes, I would. I understand clearly what you have told me." And they prayed together.

Rudy told us later that Udchus was "just like rice ready for harvesting."

Next time we saw Udchus he was smiling broadly. He told us what he had done and added, "When the Mallango people see how much I've changed they'll be asking, 'Who is this new Udchus?'"

Then he looked me squarely in the eye and said, "I'm so glad you and Judith and your family came to Mallango. I never imagined I would ever see books written in my language, and now we even have part of the Bible. I want this translation of Mark to be the best possible. I want every Kalinga to understand it. When I return home, I will share it with my people."

Udchus returned to Mallango ahead of us, promising to continue helping us when we arrived. But he wasn't there when we arrived and no one could tell us why. Two days later a letter from him told us he was in Tabuk, the provincial capital, for some reason he didn't mention. The note started, "Bruce and Judith, I praise the Lord that I wasn't there at the exact time I said I would be."

A little perplexed by this opening statement, we read on: "Have somebody else continue the translation in my absence, and I will help you when I come home. Don't worry about me. I still think about the Lord Jesus Christ. God bless you, and may His Spirit help you to do your work of translation."

We were disappointed that he wasn't available straight away, but at least Saryong would be working with us.

We were in for further disappointment. He was too busy.

A month after returning to Mallango, Udchus had still not returned, no one else was willing to help us, and we were feeling extremely discouraged again.

Another Balangao Bible Conference

Easter 1977: It was time for the annual Balangao Bible Conference. Surprisingly, twelve Mallango men said they wanted to go. We didn't realise there was that much interest in the Gospel. However, although we wanted to let them all go, only nine could fit on the two flights we had requested.

We needn't have been stressed about who would go and who wouldn't. Thirty minutes before the first plane was due, all but one, Domingo, Saryong's uncle who lived up at the road, had backed out. When he arrived at the airstrip and found he was the only one going, he began looking for reasons why he couldn't go either.

"Many heads have been rolled by Balangaos in the past," he said. "I'm not ready to add mine!" With our assurance that they had changed their ways, he decided that since he'd come this far, if we could convince some others to accompany him, he'd go. He wanted a ride in the plane, anyway.

We were disappointed that Saryong didn't want to go, but managed to convince three other men with adventurous spirits to go. One of them, Marnawa, an old man well respected in the community, said, "I'll go. I want to ride in the plane too!" As he was climbing in, he heard someone saying that the conference would last five days. "But I thought it was only one day," he protested loudly, and started to get out.

In a flash of "inspiration," the pilot pushed him back onto the seat and shut the door. Marnawa protested but he couldn't work out how to open the door. He reluctantly agreed to go. He came home believing in Christ.

Meanwhile, there was still room for one passenger, and my Scottish ancestry wouldn't allow me to let a seat that was paid for leave empty. I had to find someone to fill that seat. Anyone. Looking around, the first person I saw was Ammoya. I asked him if he would like to go and he immediately replied, "Yes!"

Quitting Time

As soon as the words came out of my mouth I wanted to kick myself. I thought, Why in the world did I ask him? We've wasted our money after all. We had rarely seen Ammoya sober, so there really seemed no point in him going. But it was too late. The invitation had been given and he had accepted. We had to let him go.

He also came back believing! On their return to Mallango all five delegates were bubbling over with excitement about the conference. "Questions, questions, questions; day and night plus!" Marnawa said.

"We didn't sleep the whole time," Domingo added. "People were continually coming to talk with us. Before I didn't know what to think about this belief of my nephew Saryong, but now my mind is very open—it's open to heaven. Before when Saryong tried to explain to me about God, I didn't believe what he said. But now that I've been to the conference, and heard many others explain about God exactly as Saryong did, I'll be able to believe when he talks to me again."

Allig said, "I saw the difference that the Word of God has made to the Balangao people. We Mallango people also need the Bible in our language!"

Ammoya said, "I want a Holy Bible, in English, so I can learn more." I gave him a copy of the Good News Bible. Originally produced for readers whose second language is English, I thought it would be easier for him to read than most English versions. "No," he protested, handing it back. "I want a Holy Bible."

I was curious. What was he talking about? It turned out that an English Bible he had seen in Balangao had the words Holy Bible on its cover, so that's what he wanted. No other title would satisfy him.

Reluctantly, because I knew his English was limited, I gave him a copy of the Revised Standard Version Holy Bible and he began to study it. Day after day he would sit reading, and then he would tell his neighbours, and anyone else who would listen, what he had learned.

Encouragements and otherwise

In April 1977 we finished the first draft translation of John's Gospel, and Udchus began studying it with us to improve it where needed. The work was going well, and of course Judith and I were keen to get it finished so the people would have more of the Good News about Jesus to read. But without explanation, Udchus suddenly stopped coming to work. We didn't see him for over a week. Then when we noticed him some distance away in the village, he appeared to see us and then turned and walked away. Next morning we heard that he had left Mallango and gone to Tabuk again.

I asked Palongpong if he thought we might have done something to offend Udchus, and he commented that it had been puzzling him too that Udchus hadn't come to work for a while. Then we realised that Saryong hadn't been to our house for nearly two weeks either. What was going on?

One morning I was surprised to see Udchus in the village. We didn't even know he had returned to Mallango. When I asked him about helping with the translation again, he seemed very evasive and said he would be going to Manila in two or three days.

A week later he was still in Mallango but still not working with us. So I asked him, "Would you please help me for just three weeks so we can finish the translation of John's Gospel?" He looked down at the ground for what seemed minutes, then without looking at me he said, "I'll ask my brother-in-law to help you." Then he turned and walked away. I felt discouraged as I watched him disappear into his house.

His brother-in-law showed no interest at all in working with us, but two days later we received some very welcome encouragement from another source. We noticed Allig reading an English New Testament and looking up references he had noted at the Balangao Bible Conference. He was finding the English difficult, so I gave him a New Testament in the trade language, Ilocano, and he found that easier to understand.

"I want to learn," he said with obvious enthusiasm, "and I also want to be baptised. I want to tell others what I've learned, too, so that more will believe in God."

Later Domingo came and talked with us for three hours. He told us he also believed and that he wanted to grow in his faith.

Next day Ammoya told us about his faith in the Lord Jesus, and of how hungry he was to read the Scriptures. "It was when I read the draft of the Gospel of Mark in my own language that I understood and put my faith in the Lord Jesus Christ," he said. "Now I want to learn about living as a Christian. But all I have is the English Bible you gave me. It's hard to understand. I need you to do your translation work quickly."

We had a lot to be encouraged about after all, but we were still discouraged. We had been back in the village for six weeks and still had no translation helper.

However, ten days after Ammoya's plea that we translate the Scriptures quickly, he himself offered to help finish the revision of John's Gospel, "to make sure it says what it's supposed to say." Palongpong joined us too. We made excellent progress, and by the end of the first day we were all thoroughly exhausted.

That wonderful day working together was followed by several more wonderful days—all exhausting but all productive—as we read through the entire draft. Then we read it again, slowly and carefully, verse by verse, over several more days. Our goal was to produce a really good final draft that could be checked by a translation consultant.

Meanwhile, the Gospel of Mark was at the printer, and in May 1977, 100 copies of that book arrived—the first Scripture portion published in the Southern Kalinga language. It was a special moment for us when we unpacked it.

Our enthusiasm was not shared by many others. Interest among the people was low. Only a handful wanted a copy.

Food for some thought

There's very little space near the village to grow food. People plant beans and other vegetables on whatever available space there is, but that's usually on the side of a hill. Some have been badly hurt when they have fallen over in their gardens because their fall was several metres down. Occasionally one dies from a fall or a landslide while working in his garden.

One of our favourite meats was dog. The first time we tried it was the hardest. It just didn't want to go down, even with onions. Just before we came home to Australia for our first major break, we were having lunch in the SIL guesthouse in Manila. The main course was noodles with pieces of pork. When Judith and I noticed that David and Elizabeth weren't eating the meat, just pushing it around on their plates, we told them to eat up. Elizabeth looked at us and said, "We don't like pig." And David added, "We only like dog." We told them not to mention that little fact when we were in Australia!

Another major culinary experience was with the heart of a carabao (water buffalo). On several occasions we were kindly given a whole heart by a family who had butchered a carabao. The first time we tried it, it was hard to tackle wholeheartedly, but we persisted and came to enjoy it, especially when fried with onions. A heart usually provided us with enough meat for about five days.

Another "taste experience" was with the *araka*, a large red ant served up in sizes ranging from newly-hatched to ready to leave the nest. Everything was boiled, including the larva, which was also eaten. It wasn't at all meaty, however, and was a little scratchy on the way down the throat.

Quitting Time

I was once given part of the stomach, complete with undigested grass, but I couldn't stomach that either. We also tried dog liver—it was okay, but certainly not our favourite delicacy.

Every year, all the chickens in the village died from a disease referred to as "the pest." Our only chicken was a victim of the disease, but it wasn't wasted. After it died our neighbours ate it.

One afternoon we heard that the Regional Director of Schools, Dr. Sanchez, and his assistant, Mr. Mendoza, and other education officials would be in Lubuagan, about three hours' hike away. They were attending a conference with all the teachers from the municipalities of Tinglayan, Tanudan and Lubuagan. Seeing it as a good opportunity to share what we were doing, I accompanied the Mallango schoolteachers who formed part of the Tinglayan contingent.

During the afternoon program, the chairman introduced all the visiting dignitaries and school officials, and then added, "There is also one here from abroad whom I should introduce, because he, with his wife, is also doing his bit for the education of the Kalingas, Mr. Bruce Grayden." A big ovation followed. It was a bit embarrassing.

Later I was invited to eat at the table of the distinguished visitors. It was quickly becoming dark and everyone was hungry, so we decided to eat without waiting for the lamps to be lit. I sampled a little from several plates of food—cautiously—because I didn't recognise much in the dark. I didn't fancy eating the "spare parts" of animals, or meat with a lot of fat. When I found something that tasted good, I decided to venture no further and piled my plate with it, then sat down to eat just the one dish. That seemed a safe plan for me since my stomach was so sensitive.

I had almost finished my plateful when the lamps were lit. I was shocked to discover that I was eating pig fat with thick gravy of cooked blood! I didn't line up for seconds.

Roman Catholic missionaries have worked in Southern Kalinga for several decades. In his book, *Mountain Arbiters*, William Dozier notes: "Since 1920, three denominations—one Roman Catholic and two Protestant—have served the Kalinga population. The number of actual converts is minimal—the Kalinga have not embraced Christianity in vast numbers. The area is extremely rugged, almost inaccessible during the rainy season, and missionary personnel have been entirely inadequate in numbers to serve such a mountainous population."

The only priest in the municipality lived at Tinglayan, and he visited Mallango perhaps once each year. One day he came and married eighteen couples. One couple already had eleven children. Most adults were already married under local custom, but when people are also married by the priest, their children can be baptised and get a baptismal certificate, which is helpful for proving their age and identity if they want to apply for a job in the city later.

After the service I was invited with most of the village men to the home of one of the happy couples to eat the "spare parts" of a water buffalo that had been butchered for the occasion. My share included part of a lung. Wishing I was somewhere else at that moment—anywhere would do— I put it gingerly into my mouth and chewed it.

It was like rubber. I kept chewing it for about ten minutes, managing to get it part way down my throat several times, but it kept coming back up. I gave up. I just couldn't swallow it. I began to consider what might be an appropriate course of action in this culture for such a situation.

Hoping no one would notice lest someone be offended, I carefully removed the piece of lung from my mouth and placed it on the edge of my plate. The old man beside me picked it up, said, "This looks well chewed," put it in his mouth, and swallowed it! He was grateful because he had no teeth. I lost what little appetite I might have had for anything else.

Quitting Time

I had no appetite either for the tadpoles I was offered another time. However, listening to my heart rather than my head, and seeing this as a way of expressing my appreciation for Emilio's hospitality and friendship, I ate them.

I should have listened to my head. Those slimy, gritty creatures, which started their life in rice fields fertilised by manure from water buffaloes, signalled the beginning of a problem with amoebic dysentery, which I've never been able to shake off.

On another occasion when we were offered tiny snail-like shells from the rice fields, I declined as graciously as I could, with respect for those who offered them. Judith, however, accepted their offer and quickly acquired a taste for the little meat inside the shells and the art of sucking it out, which looks and sounds like a kiss.

The twenty-eighth of September 1977 was a day for great rejoicing by us: Victoria accepted the Lord. We were in Bagabag for another workshop with Victoria as our house helper. Virgie, a lady from Barlig working as a translation assistant for Dave and Joan Ohlson, led her to the Lord.

A month later a friend from Australia, Claire, arrived to visit us and a couple of other colleagues. While talking with Victoria one day, Claire asked about her hopes and dreams. Victoria told her she had graduated from high school—accomplished by only a minority of Mallango children. She wanted to go to college to become a schoolteacher, but since her parents couldn't afford to support her any longer, she couldn't fulfil her dream. Claire offered to support her through college.

A grateful Victoria had almost completed her bachelor of arts degree and was thinking about applying for a teaching position when we felt that God was prompting us to talk with her. We told her we believed that God had more than teaching in His plan for her and that she should consider going on to

Bible college. Claire agreed to continue her support, so Victoria applied to study at the Philippine Baptist Theological Seminary in Baguio. Three years later she graduated with a master of divinity.

Believing God was guiding her further, she applied and was accepted as a member of the Translators Association of the Philippines and began work in translation and literacy in Lubuagan, the language group a little north of hers.

Emma's birth

Early in October 1977, we were happy to leave the constant mix of frustrations and joys that was our experience in Mallango to return to Bagabag. We had a special reason to do that. Our baby was due that month.

October 21 turned out to be both special and unforgettable. That Emma Louise was born was special. It was the circumstances of her birth that were unforgettable.

Shortly after labour pains began at about 1:30 a.m., Judith remarked casually, "I think our baby will be born later today." One minute later she decided it would be sooner rather than later. I ran to the home of colleagues Winston and Lois Churchill to get their Ford Bronco, which we'd arranged to borrow. I then woke our neighbour, Tom Headland, who had offered to stay with the children when the time came.

We set off for the clinic at Lamut seven kilometres away. Little more than a kilometre from home, the engine stalled and wouldn't restart. This couldn't be happening, we thought—this was real life, not a movie!

As I pushed the vehicle to the side of the road, Judith called out, "I don't think I can wait any longer!" So I helped her onto the back seat, and within seconds Emma was born.

Surprisingly to us, we didn't panic. As far as Judith could tell, everything about the baby seemed normal. We had one problem, however—we couldn't see her...or him! I couldn't find the interior light switch, and there was no moonlight.

Quitting Time

The light from a handful of stars was sufficient only to allow us to see each other as very dim silhouettes, but we couldn't make out features.

We prayed aloud and trusted God that all would be well.

After a few minutes we concluded that no one was likely to come along at that hour of the night who might get help for us. There was no alternative but for me to run back to the Churchills' home and tell them about our predicament. With what seemed a feeble attempt to make Judith and the baby as comfortable as possible, I reluctantly set off to run back to Bagabag.

There wasn't enough starlight to see the concrete road. Each time I strayed from it I slid in the gravel beside the road. Fortunately I kept my balance and didn't fall over. Within ten minutes I had found the Churchills' house and was knocking loudly on their front door and calling out to them.

Winston, wondering who was making such a racket at 2 o'clock in the morning, quickly appeared in the doorway. He looked relieved as he recognised me. The curious look that followed changed as I blurted out, "Judith's just had a baby! She's in the Bronco about a kilometre from here! The engine has conked out and I can't start it!"

He ran to his motorbike, shouting, "Jump on behind me." We were soon back at the Bronco. After assurances from Judith that she and the baby seemed okay, Winston reached under the dashboard and turned on the interior light. Checking the fuel gauge, he discovered the fuel had been switched to the reserve tank, which was empty. He changed it over to the main fuel tank, which was full, and then I drove Judith to the clinic at Lamut while Winston followed on his motorbike in case something else went wrong.

The clinic was in darkness, but hearing my loud knocking, the doctor and six nurses quickly appeared. The generator was started and the umbilical cord was cut. Then Judith climbed out of the Bronco and walked into the clinic, while all the nurses stood in a row to one side watching in awe. One of them observed admiringly, "She's so strong!"

When everything was done, Dr Belarde looked at me, chuckled, and said, "You did a great job as the 'mid-husband,' Bruce!"

Judith and Emma stayed in the clinic till early afternoon. Then, since mother and baby seemed fine, and no one was looking after them anyway, we went home. The doctor charged us $25 for the "delivery," although we couldn't work out why!

A literacy team

One of the encouraging events of 1977 was the arrival of a literacy team. Most men could read, but less than a third of adult women could and we wanted the women to be able to read the Scriptures too. We were happy to have some help with the literacy task, so we invited Carol Porter and Rosalie Bulmer to come and set up a literacy program. They were later joined by Pam Memory. During the next three years these three literacy specialists were able to enthuse many of the women to learn to read and they also taught twenty men and women to be teachers of adult literacy.

When they left the project, several gave testimony to their help. Ammoya said, "We are very grateful to God for sending the ladies to teach those who didn't know how to read. Because of their good work, all the adults in the first classes can now read the Gospel of John which has been translated into our language."

Kawi said, "We are so happy that we have learned to read and write because now we can see for ourselves what God's Word says."

I want to quit!

Although our determination to get the job done saw us make good progress on translation—the Gospels of Mark and John were completed and published within three and a half years of our arrival in Mallango—instead of being encouraged we were becoming more and more discouraged the longer we were there. Our minds were often taken off the good things that were happening.

Adding to our difficulties was the persistent opposition towards us from some people. It was all taking its toll on us, particularly me. Towards the end of 1977, when I told Saryong we would be going back to Australia for furlough, he remarked, "When you go home you may as well stay there because no one else here is ever going to believe."

For me that was the final blow. It was too hard for me. I wanted to quit.

Around that time the Australian Director of Wycliffe, David Cummings, was in the Philippines running a workshop for members preparing for furlough. We had attended a previous workshop so were not at this one. However, we happened to meet up with David and I poured out my feelings to him.

"David," I burst out, "I want to quit!" He looked surprised but let me go on. "I'm sick more often than I'm well. Our son David has had TB. When our children are sick in the village, it's so difficult to get medical attention; I don't think it's right to keep my little family here. The people don't want us anyway. They're not interested in what we're...."

David interrupted me. "Tell me," he said, "has there been any response at all in the three years you've been here?"

"Yes," I replied, hesitantly. "Seven people have believed."

Grabbing me by the shoulders David said, "Bruce, what are you talking about? That's so beautiful! You say they don't want you here, that they aren't interested in what you're doing, and there are already seven believers? That's magnificent! There are lots of churches back home that haven't seen seven people come to Christ in forty years!"

Instead of leaving for Australia, we decided to go back to the village for another year. It was a year we will never forget.

SEVEN

Worth Waiting For

A surprise on our return

On January 6, 1978 we returned to Mallango. We had a good break over the Christmas period and felt we could just about handle another year before furlough, or so we hoped. Palongpong got us off to a good start at the airstrip with his report that the Mallango people had celebrated Christmas for the first time. He encouraged them to continue the practice, "Now that we know God."

We were curious. What was he talking about? Apart from the seven we knew about, who knew God? Later in the day we saw Domingo, one of the believers, and asked him what the people had done at Christmas time. "The whole village feasted," he replied. "The few who are believing provided the meat, and everyone else brought rice and vegetables. It was a happy time." We were amazed at the initiative the believers had taken and were sorry we hadn't been there to celebrate with them.

Two mornings later Ammoya and his neighbour Pannokan, both in their mid-fifties, came to our house. After chatting for a couple of hours, they finally got around to the main reason they had come to see us. Ammoya said, "While you were away on your vacation, I had Bible studies with Pannokan and led him to the Lord."

We must have looked a little odd to them as our mouths fell open and tears began to fill our eyes. "I was baptised when I was an infant," Pannokan informed us, "but throughout my whole life I have followed our traditional customs, looking to

119

the spirits to help me. It was while reading the Scriptures that I realised I had never really understood about Jesus Christ. I can see that I can't have true faith in the Lord if I'm still obeying the evil spirits through our old customs. I didn't have true faith in Jesus Christ before. Now I do."

Ammoya then said, "Although I was baptised as a child, is it wrong that I want to be baptised again, now that I'm believing?" I gave a simple reply: "No, it's not wrong."

Then Ammoya surprised us even more. "As we studied the Scriptures together," he added, "we felt more and more that we believers should be encouraging and supporting each other. It seemed to us that there would be value in all the believers meeting together for prayer and Bible study. Are we wrong in thinking that?"

We could hardly believe our ears. We had often thought how we would love to start a Bible study. We had even felt guilty that we hadn't. After all, we were the only missionaries there—why weren't we doing our "job" by starting a church? It was so hard watching the first believers struggle with the insensitivity of some people towards them, and we had so much wanted to correct that. We knew it would greatly encourage them if they were to meet together to study the Scriptures and to pray for each other. We wanted to suggest many things, but we hadn't because we felt strongly that we should not be the ones to start a church. God Himself would prompt them as they read His Word in their own language.

We weren't totally confident that would happen, but we were certainly hoping and praying it would—sometime.

Many Kalinga people felt that Christianity was a "Western" religion. They had already been given a strong taste of outside religion; several sects had come to Mallango over the years. Some people had accepted the new teachings, but each time within a year their followers had become disillusioned, the groups had disbanded, and the people had vowed never to be tricked again—until the next sect or cult came along.

One older man told us the same would happen if we started a church, and many had agreed with him. "We have our god already. Why should we be looking for another one?"

Since they still depended on the customs they had always known, they needed to see that Christianity was not just another religion or sect that they might be talked into accepting.

It occurred to us that if we were the ones to start a church and later for some reason had to leave, never to return—although at the time that seemed completely hypothetical—the church might collapse if it had been built around our leadership.

We felt inadequate for the task ourselves anyway. We could identify with the apostle Paul when he said in 1 Corinthians 2:3–5, "I came to you in weakness—timid and trembling. And my message and my preaching were very plain. I did not use wise and persuasive speeches, but the Holy Spirit was powerful among you. I did this so that you might trust the power of God rather than human wisdom." (NLT)

Therefore, we had not organized anything, but we asked our prayer partners back home to pray that the believers would soon see the need to meet together for Bible study and fellowship. We told them we wanted a church to start, but it had to come through the believers, through their study of the Scriptures, and through their relationship with the Lord.

And now Ammoya and Pannokan were talking about it.

I said to them, "It's a good idea," and said no more. Judith and I wanted to jump up and hug them, and say, Yes! Come to our house next Sunday, and we'll have a Bible study. This is what we've been waiting for! Instead, we just looked at each other, broad grins on our faces and a million thoughts racing through our heads.

Domingo, one of the other believers, dropped by later that day. After we had chatted for a while, he invited us to his home the following Sunday. We were hesitant about accepting his invitation because we wouldn't be able to have our special Sunday morning family devotions where our children always took part. However, we often had to snatch time when we could because many villagers stayed home from the fields to rest on Sundays so several would come to our house to talk with us.

Since we wanted to encourage Domingo, we accepted his invitation. When he listed the names of all the other believers, we looked at each other—our mouths open once again.

To add to our excitement, later in the day Saryong said to us, "While you were away I thought very seriously about baptism, and I've decided that even if I'm the only one, I want to be baptised." Then he added that his nephew Domingo would probably also want to be baptised, and that we could discuss it next Sunday.

It was all rather overwhelming! We heard things that day that we had been longing to hear since we'd first arrived in Mallango.

Two days later Ammoya and Pannokan led yet another older man to the Lord.

Sunday came—the fifteenth of January 1978. The long hike to Domingo's home required cautious navigation down the narrow mountain trail around rice terraces, followed by a steep climb to Mallango's small daughter-village, Char-ig. Along with a dozen curious onlookers, all but one of the believers were already there, including our literacy team, Carol, Rosalie and Pam.

A week earlier it had been hard to believe our ears. This time it was our eyes that were affected. As we sat down Ammoya said, "It's good that we who have been convinced by God's Word have grouped ourselves to study it together."

We were nervous, but excited. We talked together for over three hours, broke for lunch, then talked for another two.

We sang songs translated into the language. Then they asked me to speak briefly, and followed up with lots of questions and discussion. We struggled; many of their questions were hard to answer. Their deep questions were about sin, sacrificing, living as a Christian in their culture, and about what they could expect in the future. They were so keen to learn.

It was wonderful listening to them talk about their faith, about what the Lord meant to them now that they knew Him. They discussed the matter of their baptism, but didn't reach a decision as to who would be baptised or when. They also discussed the stand they considered they should take as believers in their community.

Someone suggested having regular Bible studies, and they decided to meet together every Sunday. The next time they wanted me to give a Bible study—not just questions and answers and discussion, like this first occasion, but a "real" Bible study. Saryong requested that we first study what they as believers should do now that they were believing. Then we all returned to our homes.

What a day that was—a day we'd prayed and longed for. The believers had met together for the first time, and it had been instigated by them.

More surprises

The second Sunday approached and I was reminded several times that I was to bring a study from God's Word to the believers. I knew I shouldn't take any leadership role. I was certain I wasn't fluent enough in the language to lead a Bible study, but they were so desperate to learn that I agreed to their request. I prepared a study on obedience.

The "church" had grown that week. The thirty that came to the second Bible study held in Saryong's home included 18 curious onlookers.

As we all sat on the floor—Saryong's whole house was only as big as an average dining room back home—all eyes focused on me as they waited for the Bible study to begin. I suddenly felt uncomfortable. I thought, I shouldn't be the one to do this! So I picked up my notes and my Bible, put them in front of Saryong sitting next to me, and said, "You must do it!"

"I couldn't do it," he protested. "I'm unqualified, and anyway, I have nothing prepared." But after further coaxing he said, "Okay, I'll try."

He was nervous at first, but as he proceeded with the study he became more and more animated. When he finished the study three hours later, this unqualified and unprepared man was sitting almost in the centre of the room in his enthusiasm.

In addition to confirming that they wanted to meet every week, the believers were convinced that God had selected Saryong to be their teacher. They never asked me to lead a Bible study again.

From that time on, Sunday services consisted of singing, testimonies, prayer, and a very long study, interrupted by anyone who had something to add to the speaker's words.

Services started when a fair number of people were there, and usually lasted about three hours. No one took any notice of the time until a few months later when some of the leaders were invited to a training workshop run by another mission. They came back and reported, "We've been doing it the wrong way! Services should start on time, and last for only one hour. Plus the teacher should speak without interruption!"

The first time they tried conducting services the "right" way, they decided it was too restrictive and immediately reverted to the way they enjoyed.

A week after the second service in Mallango, some of the believers said they wanted to be baptised, and they asked me to baptise them. Reluctant because I didn't want to take such a role in the church, I said, "Why not let Saryong or Ammoya baptise you? They are very godly men."

But Ammoya said, "No, my friend. We couldn't do it. No one in the village would want us to baptise them. They've known us all their lives. They know all our sins, all our faults, what we've been like in the past. They wouldn't consider it right if we who are no better than them are the ones to baptise them. As for you, they don't know your past. They will let you baptise them."

Quickly searching for another solution, I said to him, "What would you think about calling the Balangao elders to come and baptise you?" They agreed and so did the Balangao elders when asked. Three offered to come.

Just before the plane bringing the Balangao elders arrived, we heard that no one was willing to be baptised after all. Palongpong said, "I want to understand better first, and I also need to repent of my past wrongdoings." Saryong and Victoria decided they would wait a while. Domingo wasn't even home. These were the people we thought would be first in line for baptism.

We were disappointed, but the Balangao elders decided to stay for the weekend anyway. Fanganan said he would teach from the Scriptures to anyone who would listen.

By Sunday morning, five men wanted to be baptised— the five oldest believers: Kissub (67), Atas (59), Marnawa (59), Ammoya (56) and Pannokan (56). Fanganan carefully quizzed them to be sure they understood what they were doing.

The nearest water deep enough for immersing a person was a brook about 15 minutes' hike away. Word about the event quickly spread, and there was quite a procession as dozens of people walked single file along the narrow trail around the edges of the rice terraces to the brook.

Atas was the first to wade into the cold, swiftly flowing water. One of the Balangao elders prayed, and then Fanganan baptised Atas. The other four followed. It was very moving watching those five village elders making a public display of their faith.

Saryong later explained to us why he wasn't baptised this time. "I wanted the old men to be the first baptised," he said. "They will show the way to the rest of the village. In this society the old people are the ones with the most respect. It's they who make the rules. Therefore, it could prove extremely significant that old men set the standard by being the first baptised."

The believers decided to butcher a large pig "so that the rest of the village can join in our happiness." They cooked two, and over 600 people came to the feast.

Saryong suggested that he and I should meet on Friday nights with Domingo and the five men who had been baptised, for prayer and Bible study, to prepare for the services on Sundays. He felt they should all share in the ministry.

The following Friday eleven men and four women came to our place for the first Friday night Bible study. We studied Mark 1:1–20. Saryong led most of the study, and was wonderful.

Next morning, Kissub shared with us how every night since his baptism he'd had dreams where the spirits of dead relatives were calling him. The dreams reminded him of the experience of his sister some years before. She had been sick for several weeks when one night the spirit of her dead husband spoke to her in a dream. He told her he was going to another province to get some pigs and two weeks later he would return with them. Everyone knew the significance of her dream. She was going to die—and exactly two weeks after her dream, she died.

Judith and I prayed with Kissub and encouraged him to pray before he slept that night. Before breakfast next morning he was back at our house reporting that he hadn't dreamed at all during the night, and that he had woken up feeling refreshed. Every other morning since his baptism, he'd woken up feeling like he'd been working all night.

Fourteen came to the second Friday night Bible study. Saryong's study went for three hours. He was marvellous, and we felt privileged listening to him. A month after Sunday services began, 45 adults were attending them. There were already 24 believers.

Two months later, Saryong drank a little too much wine at a village celebration and had to sleep it off. Next morning was a Sunday. When he woke up he felt ashamed, feeling he'd let everyone down, including God. However, wanting to fulfil his responsibility of preaching and teaching God's Word, he asked God to forgive him and to speak through him despite his indiscretion. As he walked to the place where the service would be held, some people taunted him, saying, "Ha! Here comes the leader of the believers, drunk one day and preaching the next. How can this be?"

He never drank again!

Three months after the church started, there were 62 adults at the morning service. That Sunday Saryong taught from Mark 12. He called on me several times to help him explain some verses, but I think he was just being polite since he didn't really need to—his understanding was excellent.

At the end of the service, I asked what needs each one had and tried to encourage them to pray. Up to that time only Saryong and Ammoya had prayed aloud in public, but this time Domingo and Palongpong also prayed. It was great hearing them talking aloud to God for the first time. We felt that God was pretty pleased about it, too.

A week later another 20 believers, 9 men and 11 women, were baptised. This time we went to a coffee grove further upstream from the previous site and the men dammed up the brook, then scooped out dirt and rocks to make it deep enough to baptise.

There were now 61 believers, and 26 of them had been baptised. In my diary I wrote Mark 12:11, "This is the Lord's doing, and it is marvellous to see." (NLT) It certainly was.

Arakoy, a man of about 50, had come to the service for the first time that day. Later he said, "I didn't come before because I thought I already knew about God. But when I listened today, I realised I didn't really know about Him at all. What I heard sounded like the truth."

One of the men baptised was Awingan, a man in his early thirties. He gave this testimony: "For a while I thought the reason the Grayden family came here was to buy our words and make money from them. When some of the Balangaos came here to make God's Word known to the people, I spoke badly to them, calling them killers.

"It's true that they were once killers. As warriors they would kill a man and then dance around the body. I wanted nothing to do with those that came to teach God's Word in our village. In fact, I resented them being here so much that I was ready to kill them if they talked to me about Jesus Christ. None did, but my curiosity was aroused.

"One day I went near to where they were teaching so I could listen. I couldn't understand why I would do that. Perhaps it was God who changed my mind. I felt ashamed to let them see me because of what I had been saying about them, but I wanted to listen.

"I understood a little, and I went and asked Bruce if he had a Bible that I could read, even English. He said, 'Yes, I have one.' So I borrowed it and I began to read it that day.

"Then the Balangao visitors invited us to their next Bible Conference, and I was one of the nine who went from Mallango. There were many hundreds of people at the conference from many places. I listened very carefully to all the messages, and it came to my mind that maybe I am one of those who will be thrown away (sent to hell).

"So I kept reading the Bible, and I began to change. The bad things I used to say and do became less. When others said bad things to me, instead of responding like I used to, I tried to just keep quiet. Sometimes I said something bad when it was too hard for me to bear what they were saying, but I know it's not possible to change all at once."

"One Sunday when I heard the Word of God taught, I knew it was the truth, and I believed in Jesus Christ. And now many that I speak to about Him also turn to Him. What we have to do is tell people about the Lord, and although some will not listen, some will listen.

"In the past our custom was to believe in omens such as the call of the ichaw bird, a certain bark of the dog, a certain squeal of the pig, and sneezing. Now we have read God's Word in our own language. John 14:1 tells us that we should not worry about anything. We should believe in Jesus and in God who sent Him here to this earth.

"We who are learning His Word from the time we were baptised put aside the customs of our ancestors. We don't believe in them any more because we know it's not them that will save us. For God's Word tells us that it is only through Jesus Christ that we will be saved."

That evening Saryong overheard some teenagers talking about the believers. They were saying, "Maybe this belief they have is true! Look at Awingan! He used to yell and scream at his family every night, and often in his temper he would go outside with his *bolo* (machete) to spear and disturb his neighbours. But he does none of that any more. He's completely changed!"

Saryong was encouraged. So were we!

By the first Sunday in May, over 80 adults were attending the services. During that morning's service, Imakay, a woman in her thirties, told how the previous evening she had talked to a teenager who had wanted to commit suicide. She told him simply, "You should change your thoughts from bad to God!" Right there and then she prayed for him, and he changed his mind about suicide. Imakay saw that as a miracle.

Another 21 were baptised that afternoon—two men and nineteen women.

EIGHT
New Experiences

Ammoya

W e had rarely seen Ammoya sober. However, after attending the Balangao Bible conference in 1977, Ammoya was a changed man. Every time I saw him he was studying the Bible. Some of the villagers ridiculed him, "You'll go crazy reading so much."

His faith was severely tested when his only daughter, ten-year-old Anchayaw, died. We were away at the time and arrived back in Mallango the day after her funeral. We couldn't help feeling that we had let Ammoya and Lumay down by not being there when they had such great sorrow, but of course we knew nothing about it until our return to Mallango.

They only had two children, and now their daughter was dead. We felt crushed by her unexpected death and knew that her parents would be even more so.

Anchayaw had fallen ill quite suddenly, and no one knew the cause. When her condition began to deteriorate, Lumay, who didn't share Ammoya's faith in God, pleaded with him to let her call Ampug, the shaman. "Ampug will be able to determine which spirits are causing our little girl's illness," she begged.

"No!" Ammoya said firmly. "I won't allow anything to do with the spirits in our home any more."

"Will you just let Anchayaw die?" Lumay cried, wiping her daughter's fevered brow. "Why can't we do what we have always done?"

New Experiences

"Satan is trying to destroy my faith," Ammoya declared. "I will not give in to him. I will trust God. The power of the spirits is great, but God's power is greater." But even as he said these words, he was being torn apart inside.

Although Anchayaw's condition steadily deteriorated, Ammoya's conviction that he should not call the shaman strengthened. He was sure God would heal their daughter. When he realised she was indeed dying, he couldn't bear to look at the accusing eyes of his wife. The many relatives and friends who crowded into their home added to his agony. While they all watched, some wailing, others sobbing, Anchayaw died.

At that moment, to the amazement of all the onlookers, particularly those sitting beside her body, the section of floor on which Anchayaw lay dropped about 30 centimetres—then immediately it returned to its normal position as if some unseen hand was holding up the floor.

Some of the men crawled under the house to repair the supports holding up the floor, but they found them all quite sound. When they reported this to the grieving crowd, one said, "It's a sign that the spirits are angry." But Ammoya declared, "I don't understand it, but I believe it's really a sign from God. He wants me to remain strong in my faith, like these floor supports—you can see for yourselves that they should have been broken but they are still strong."

When we asked Ammoya how he was, he told us, "Of course I'm sad. I miss our beautiful daughter but I am not discouraged. No! My faith in God is stronger than ever!"

We wondered what Lumay thought about all this and prayed for her often during the days that followed. Surprisingly, Lumay also seemed to be coping extremely well.

We had found Lumay difficult to get to know during our early years in Mallango. We had never seen her smile. Shy and withdrawn, she had always tried to avoid us. On the rare occasions we did meet, she always quickly covered her face with her

hands and mumbled from behind tightly closed fingers.
Her hands hid ugly scars on her nose and chin, legacies of a
murder attempt by her first husband, who in a drunken rage
slashed her with his machete and then killed their two children
before killing himself.

One morning shortly after Anchayaw's death, Judith was
walking past their house. For the first time Judith saw Lumay
smiling with no attempt to cover her scars.

With eyes brimming with tears, Ammoya told us what had
happened. He had helped us revise the translation of John's
Gospel, and two days after Anchayaw's death some copies of
the book arrived from the publisher. Ammoya decided to use
it to teach his wife to read. Each night he read verses to her,
praying silently that God would speak to her through His
Word. He patiently guided her through the text, teaching her
to identify words, phrases and sentences until she mastered
them. As she learned to read, she understood the message
about Jesus' love and forgiveness and began to believe it was
the truth. She soon put her trust in the Lord Jesus Christ. A
remarkable change occurred in her. She no longer hid her
face; instead she looked radiant. Her horrible scars were still
there but we hardly noticed them any more. She grew quickly
in her faith.

The change in Lumay was one of many miracles that
impacted the people of Mallango and other villages.

The *chapilang*

One morning Ammoya woke earlier than usual. As
he lay there, his eyes focused on the chapilang on the wall, and
he said to himself, "Just how real is my faith in God when I let
that thing stay there? It's as if I'm serving the spirits as well as
God." He stood up, tore the chapilang from the wall, and threw
it onto the still-glowing embers of the previous evening's
cooking fire.

133

New Experiences

The *chapilang*, a frame made from wood or bamboo with an attached coconut shell bowl, was an essential element in every village home. Placed high up on an inside wall, something from every animal sacrificed by the family was put on it—the jawbone of a pig, or the leg of a hen—to "prove" to the spirits that their demands had been met.

Before we went to Mallango, two educated young men, both home from attending college in the city, had declared publicly that although the ancestors had taught them about things like the chapilang, it was just superstition and need not be followed. They removed the chapilangs from their homes.

One of the men became blind, the other lame. When they called the shaman, offered the sacrifices demanded by the spirits and replaced the chapilangs, both were instantly healed.

Early in the life of the church we had asked some of the believers about their chapilang that they all retained in their houses even after believing in God. They commented, "It doesn't mean anything to us any more. We pay no attention to it, but we'll just leave it where it is."

Though they tried to convince us otherwise, we sensed they were apprehensive about the possible consequences if they removed their chapilang. Perhaps they didn't want to deliberately provoke the wrath of the spirits—or perhaps they were afraid. They knew the spirits' power was all too real.

We wanted to tell them they could take the risk and be confident that God would protect them, but we chose to leave it to them to discover through the Word of God what they should do.

Since the two affected young men had not destroyed their chapilangs but had merely removed them from their homes, they were able to restore them to their place again. However, Ammoya hadn't thrown his chapilang out so that he could later return it to its place if he changed his mind. He had burnt it. This man, out of obedience to what he knew God's will to be, had thrown down the gauntlet to the spirits. They could try to do with him what they liked.

New Experiences

The whole village waited in fear for tragedy to strike Ammoya. He prayed that God would protect him and his family from the spirits' vengeance.

That night a woman controlled by spirits stood outside Ammoya's house and cursed all the believers. "You believers, you'll see!" she screamed. "Something terrible is going to happen to you in one month's time." She returned three more times during the night to repeat her curse.

Having witnessed the wrath of evil spirits on several occasions, we radioed our colleagues at the Bagabag centre and wrote to our supporting churches at home, asking them to pray for God's protection of the believers.

A month later to the day, all but two of the houses on the road near Mallango were shot at. After dark Domingo, one of the church elders, was seated at his kitchen table studying Scripture passages in preparation for Sunday's message. His young daughter was sitting on the table watching her father. Suddenly they heard shots fired outside their home. Domingo felt a bullet whistle past his right ear; another passed between his left arm and his chest and lodged in the table. A third also hit the table, missing his daughter's leg by a centimetre.

In the next house, Funag jumped out of bed when he heard the shots. Two bullet holes appeared where he had been lying. Bullets also came through the walls of other houses, but none of the believers nor their families were harmed. No one saw the assailants.

Soon after this incident, Pinang and her husband, Chalipug, called me to their home. "You know how Ammoya destroyed his chapilang," Pinang said. "We want to destroy ours too, and we want you to be the one to throw it onto the fire."

I felt pretty nervous about that so we prayed together and read some Scripture verses. Then feeling slightly more confident, I took the chapilang from Chalipug's hands and threw it onto the fire. It burst into flames.

New Experiences

That night Chalipug and Pinang were woken by an earthquake that shook their house. They rushed outside, expecting to see everyone else in the village joining them there, but no one did. Then looking around wide-eyed, they realised that their house was the only one shaking.

The same thing happened the following three nights. Each night the spirit who had "married" Pinang before she married Chalipug—and to which they had sacrificed a hen every month during the fifteen years of their marriage—appeared to her, demanding that another hen be sacrificed. She refused each time.

On the fifth night they called eight of the believers to their house to pray. Afterwards they went to sleep. Pinang described her sleep that night as the best she'd had in 15 years. She and her family were never bothered by spirits again.

A few weeks later Domingo burnt his chapilang. His was the third family to do this. Since none had suffered for their "breach" of the spirits' law, all the other believers decided to burn theirs too. Going from house to house, they prayed for God's protection as they removed and burnt their chapilangs. God answered their prayers. We were away from Mallango at that time but wished we could have been there to witness this milestone.

Later the believers in Arngikan village invited the Mallango believers to their village while they burnt their chapilangs. Many went. Before they removed their chapilangs from their houses, they prayed, asking God to protect them from anything bad, and God answered their prayers.

One of the believers later showed us two verses in their newly published Gospel of John (8:44 and 14:6), and they said, "Now that we believe that Jesus is the only way, we have no use for our old ways when we were always afraid of the spirits. Burning our chapilangs is one way of saying to God, 'We want to follow Your ways.' We know He'll protect us."

Even unbelievers could sense that something was different though they couldn't explain it. Some said, "It must be God's power—it's greater than that of the spirits!"

At a Sunday service in Bagabag, when Ammoya was helping us with some translation checking, he gave his testimony to our colleagues: "When I was young, I learned the Ten Commandments and memorised prayers, and then I was baptised. I never experienced anything of the work of the Spirit of God in my life. Instead I experienced the work of Satan because I was often drunk and disturbing my neighbours. I was often angry and critical of people, and slandered them.

"I obeyed the servants of Satan, the shamans. When I married my wife, we sacrificed animals to the evil spirits, and we also sacrificed pigs at the birth of our children and at other times.

"When the Grayden family first came to live in Mallango, we didn't know their purpose in coming. They told us it was about the Word of God, but we didn't understand. During their third year here some of us went to the Balangao Bible Conference.

"At that conference I heard the Gospel. They talked about Jesus Christ as the only way to God in heaven. They told how He is the truth and that He is the source of everlasting life. I understood it for the first time and knew it must be the truth. I listed all the Bible references that were given because I wanted to study them more.

"When I arrived home, Bruce asked me, 'What did you learn?' I showed him my notes and said, 'Here is what I learned; now I need a complete Bible so I can read and learn more.'

"After I got an English Bible from Bruce, I read the verses I had noted at the conference. It was good being able to read them for myself. Then I wanted to tell others what I had found. I tried to convince my neighbours about all the good things I had learned. Two of them, Pannokan and Os-ag, both old men like myself, believed. After a while, some of us believers asked Fanganan and some of his friends to come to Mallango to baptise us.

"After that I thought about the chapilang in our house and realised it was wrong to keep it. God protected me as I destroyed it.

"I know the Spirit of God has been given to me, because I have felt His work in me. My bad thoughts have been changed to good, and I no longer get angry. Knowing all these changes have taken place in me has strengthened my faith very much.

"I love you my brethren, and I thank our Father God for His love, which He has given to us here. There are very many now who are studying the Word of God and worshipping Him. Let us thank God for there is much fruit from your work here. The believers are becoming many. Let us thank our Father God and pray that it will be like this daily so that we will be many brethren in God. The believers are growing because they easily understand God's Word when our own language is read.

"We who believe His Word from the time we were baptised put aside the customs of our forefathers. We no longer believe in them; we know it is not the old customs that will save us. God's Word tells us that it is only through Jesus Christ that we will be saved. Now we pray to God to help us and bless us whom He chose as His children."

The first Sunday in July saw the biggest attendance yet at a church service—90 adults. They had been using a school classroom for several weeks, but since that was now off limits to them, they met in someone's front yard. No one was told why they were evicted from the school. One said he suspected it might have been because they spat their betel nut juice on the floor.

New Experiences

Some months later after the believers had moved into their new church building, the elders actually banned the chewing of betel nut during services—not because of the betel nut juice that was spat on the floor but because those who chewed disturbed the services when they walked around trying to borrow the ingredients from others, a nut from one, a tobacco leaf from another, and lime from yet another.

When the believers outgrew even the largest space between houses, they decided to build a simple chapel. Some donated lumber, and we offered to help pay for the roofing iron.

By early August we had translated 25 percent of the New Testament. There were over 70 believers, with 120 adults and dozens of children attending services. Saryong was teaching from the Gospel of John and doing very well. The first time he taught from John, he got through just the first five verses in three hours.

One Sunday in August Saryong announced that the following week they would elect elders and deacons. During the week Judith and I talked about his plan. We felt that since the church was so young and most of the believers were so new in their faith, few, if any, were really ready to take on such a responsibility. Therefore, we decided to "interfere." I prepared a study on the qualifications and responsibilities of elders and deacons.

The next Sunday Saryong said, "Okay, we're going to elect elders and deacons now. Who wants to suggest someone as an elder?" As names were called out, I whispered to him, "I've prepared a study on elders and deacons. Would you like me to give it?"

"No, we don't need it," he said. "Just sit down." I sat down.

Saryong wrote eight names in his notebook, including his own, then announced, "That's enough. You eight are our elders. Now, deacons?" Five names were suggested before

New Experiences

Saryong called a halt. "That's enough," he said. "We don't want the deacons to outnumber the elders. You five are all deacons." Then he went on with the rest of the service.

Since they were so young in their faith, we don't know if we would have selected many of those men for their new roles, but we conceded that they knew each other better than we did. They also knew the strength of each other's faith better than we did. As the months went by, we saw that they truly were God's choice for the task given them.

A few weeks later Saryong said to us, "Those who were chosen as elders have become very able teachers of the Word of God to the people. Therefore I'm thankful to the Father. You should also thank God for it is He who has given them their ability."

The elders sometimes asked our advice on a matter, but they didn't always take it. If they felt our advice was wrong, they weren't shy in telling us.

Several times each week the elders were called to the houses of believers to pray for sick ones. Judith and I were called to join them sometimes, but not every time.

Some unbelievers called the elders "shamans" because even though they didn't contact the spirits and no animals were sacrificed, they had in a sense taken the place of the shamans. Unbelievers ridiculed the elders if the one they prayed for didn't recover quickly, but everyone they prayed for eventually recovered from their illness within days—except Saryong's wife, Lùfay, who had TB.

Unbelievers were quick to use that fact as a way of taunting Saryong, and it hurt him. However, he clung to his faith, even when Lùfay died after three years of suffering.

By the middle of August just a few weeks later, there were 88 believers. Another 28 were baptised—17 men and 11 women. They wanted me to baptise them, so I tried to convince the elders they could do it themselves. It was part of their responsibility; they could do it just the same as I could. But they would not be persuaded. The argument that finally convinced them was over photos. Everyone wanted their photo taken as they were baptised, and I had the only camera.

"How can I baptise you," I asked them, "and take a photo of you at the same time?"

That got them thinking. "You can let Rosalie take the photos," one bright fellow said. Now how was I going to get out of that one? Then with a grin I said, "But can you imagine that Rosalie could use the camera? She's a woman!"

There was nothing more to be said—except for my apology to Rosalie for acting like the local men. She understood what I was doing, however, and I took the photos while Ammoya and Atas did the baptising.

One of the men baptised that day, Chagchag, son of the shaman Ampug, testified that he had been searching for the truth for a long time. He told how he used to entertain any "religious representative," as he called them, who came to Mallango and ask them about God. But he was never completely satisfied with their answers.

When the translation of the Gospel of John had been completed, he asked us for a copy. As he read it he felt more and more that this was the truth he was searching for. "If you hadn't given me that Gospel to read, I'd still be searching," he told us. "Now at last I have found the truth."

Làay said that she used to be a "philosophiser." She had gone to a church service with the aim of disrupting it with questions such as, "Whom did Cain marry?" She claimed she already knew God, but when she heard the Scriptures being read and taught that day she "knew that was the truth," and she believed.

Others had similar testimonies. Most said they believed because they realised that what they heard was true—it struck the right chord in their minds.

New Experiences

The Balangao elders returned to Mallango one
Friday in late August, and Fanganan taught twice each
day. Only 20–30 attended each session on the first day,
but the Saturday meetings were more encouraging with over
100 at each 3-hour session.

When they left, Fanganan reported that he was very
encouraged by the believers in Mallango. He told us,
"I believe they're hungry to learn."

In October the village councillors went to the
provincial capital, Tabuk, for the day. On the way the
believers among them said to Fatak, the husband of
Kamaw, "How impossible it is that your wife believes and you
are not even interested in the Good News! How impossible!"

Next day we saw him talking with Ammoya and others.
Within two weeks he also believed.

An experience I'd like to forget

There were several occasions when I had inadvertently caused misunderstandings with some people.
Those times were painful for me, made worse by the
fact that I rarely realised what I had done wrong; so I usually
found it impossible to repair the damage I had somehow
caused.

I will never forget one particular time I really "blew it" with
Saryong. I had spent several hours trying to fit a few translated
verses from John's Gospel to a tune common to the Mallango
people. It was frustrating getting it to work, but when it was
finally finished I felt pleased with my effort and was sure the
people would appreciate it. I went outside to test it. There
were more than a dozen men excavating for the chapel
building so I asked them to listen.

I had hardly started singing when Saryong said, "That's a
bad tune for those words!" Then he added with a sneer, "It's
not only a bad tune for those words; it couldn't be worse!"

I blurted out, "Well, you pick the best tune!" The other men could tell I was upset, so they laughed. Even though I knew that was the Kalinga way of coping with embarrassment, their reaction upset me even more. I could only think, Why are they doing this to me? Have they no respect at all for me?

I began to protest but quickly bit my bottom lip and walked away before anything else was said, by them or by me. It wasn't hard for them to tell that I was struggling.

I had a restless night, unable to sleep. My treatment of Saryong, and his of me, kept racing around in my mind. I felt miserable all the next day too and stayed away from the building site the whole day.

The following day was no better. I still felt miserable. I was disappointed that the incident had affected me so badly. I couldn't get Saryong out of my mind and didn't want to see him. In fact, I didn't want to see anyone. After lunch, realising I was overreacting badly, I went outside to face the world and help with the excavating, hoping that no one would remember what had happened a couple of days before. Several men were there including Saryong.

His welcome was cool. Within minutes he was criticising the way I was digging. Once again I couldn't believe what I was hearing. After only a few minutes I put my shovel down and left without saying a word. I couldn't take it. I needed to find a quiet place to cry.

That night when it was quite dark, I crept through the village to Ammoya's house. I broke down twice as I told him all that had happened and asked for his help and counsel as my elder.

Ammoya said, "You must forgive Saryong in the Name of the Lord Jesus Christ and forget what he has said to you." I said I would, and he said he'd pray for me. I went home feeling much better about things, and slept well.

Late the following afternoon, Ammoya asked me to go with him to Saryong's house. Most of the elders were there too.

New Experiences

As soon as I sat down, they all proceeded to tell me it was completely my fault that my relationship with Saryong had collapsed.

I tried to give my side of the story, but according to their culture I was the one at fault. For three painfully long hours I sat while they told me what I had done wrong and what I needed to do to rectify the situation. At the end, feeling quite broken, I apologised to Saryong, and he also apologised to me.

It was hard to listen to it all, particularly with the guilt I felt over my stupid actions; but in spite of the pain it caused me, I was amazed at their willingness to take their responsibility as elders so seriously that they would do what they did for me.

I've forgotten most of what they said. I sometimes wish I had taped their words or made notes afterwards—but perhaps it's better I didn't. It was a painful experience.

Why have you come here?

There was one question people asked us many times during our first few years in Mallango: "Why have you come here?" We gave the same answer every time: "We've come here to learn your language, write it down, work out the grammar, and teach people to read. Our main goal is to translate the New Testament into your language so that you can read God's message yourselves." No one quite understood, so a few weeks later we would hear the question again. "Why have you come here?"

One day an elder surprisingly said to me, "Now we know why you came here!" I said to him, "You please tell me. Why did we come here?" He gave me the identical answer we'd given so many times during those years.

Later during a church service one of the elders gave his testimony. "A few years ago a family came from another country to live here with us. Their name is Grayden. Not everyone was happy to let them stay. Some said, 'They're foreigners. Their plan is about money.' Others said, 'They will somehow take our land from us and sell it.' Still others said, 'They have just come to visit because they have extra money.'

"Then someone asked, 'Why are they learning our language?' I laughed and said, 'If they learn our language, maybe they will also learn our bad habits.'

"But all that time none of us understood their real reason for coming here until they began translating the Bible. That's when we realised their purpose—they wanted us to have the Word of God."

At last they knew!

Soon afterwards one of the elders came to us and said, "We've been reading Acts and now we feel we should be going to other places to evangelise. Is that wrong?"

I asked him, "Why do you think that might be wrong?"

"Because not everyone in our village is believing yet," he replied. "Would we be neglecting them if we go to other places to teach the Good News about Jesus?"

I answered enthusiastically, "Going to other villages is not neglecting your neighbours. It's a good idea!" After that every Sunday morning and sometimes on weekdays, we would see the elders, their copies of Mark and John under one arm and their bag of betel nut and all the other ingredients for making friends and getting a hearing under the other arm, heading off two by two to go to other villages to preach and teach the Good News.

One night, Liw-akan, a man in Man-ofar (20 minutes' hike away), was shot dead by unknown assailants. When someone had called to him from outside his house, he did not recognize the voice. Becoming suspicious, he decided to slip out the back window and get away, fearing the caller might enter and harm him. As his feet touched the ground, however, a volley of shots struck him and he died.

New Experiences

A month before while visiting Mallango, Liw-akan had attended a service. Later he started having disturbing dreams, and the night before he died he was so troubled by the dreams that he asked for a Bible to read. Unfortunately, he never did get the Bible.

Old Kissub became the first retired elder of the Mallango Bible Church. He was the only believer at the top end of the village, and his relatives had been ridiculing him so harshly that he stopped attending services. After two months' absence the other elders met and decided that Kissub would be the first "retired" elder—a nice way to do it. Then they drew lots for his replacement, and Domingo was appointed as an elder. Domingo loved reading the Bible. "These words are powerful. If people will only read them, they'll believe."

Within twelve months Domingo became the leader of the church. Saryong had asked for a break from the leadership because he couldn't take the persecution any more.

There were now 116 believers—94 in Mallango, 12 in Arngikan, and 10 in Man-ofar. The elders and others were also excited about the potential believers in Sumachor, the largest village of Southern Kalinga.

On our last Sunday in Mallango before our furlough, another 28 believers, some of them from other villages, were baptised. Among them were Ampug and Panya, both shamans.

Panya was a shaman in Arngikan. When she had believed several months before, she had renounced her spirit mediumship, but it was some time before she felt brave enough to destroy the paraphernalia connected with her work as a shaman. Even then, she and her husband Kilaw got others to do it. They asked Saryong and the elders to come, and while some prayed, others removed and burnt it all, and the Lord protected them.

New Experiences

After the baptisms the Arngikan believers invited the Mallango elders and other believers to their village to teach them more about salvation. Thirty went from Mallango, and they were very encouraged by the response from the Arngikan people to their ministry. All but one of the 80 people living there attended, and they asked many questions. They also butchered three small pigs to show their appreciation to the visitors. The only man who didn't attend the meeting was the one remaining active village shaman.

Ampug the shaman

When we first went to Mallango there were two shamans (spirit mediums), sisters Tammù and Ampug. In 1976 I asked Ampug about her role and what she thought about God and Jesus Christ. She was silent for a few seconds, then said cautiously, "I would really like to believe in them but I can't. If I stop serving the spirits, they will kill me."

When her nephew Saryong believed, she was antagonistic towards him and wouldn't let him talk about Jesus in her presence. Since Ampug was his aunt, Saryong found himself in a dilemma. On the one hand he wanted to tell people about Jesus at every opportunity; on the other hand, he didn't want to show disrespect to his aunt.

In the latter half of 1978, with the church well established, Saryong and others helped us translate some hymns and choruses and put Scripture verses to the mountain tunes that everyone knew so well. The believers loved these new songs. Children would walk around the village singing gospel songs—even the children of unbelievers. Their parents didn't stop them because they loved their own special tunes. For us it was wonderful waking up early in the morning and hearing gospel songs coming from nearby houses.

Ampug found herself listening too, and she enjoyed the singing so much that she went along to a church service just to hear the singing. She heard much more than the songs. She heard her nephew teaching about God, and to Saryong's delight, and ours, she became a believer and immediately stopped serving as a shaman.

Many of the unbelievers were angry with her. Since Tammù had already died, now they would have to walk for at least 45 minutes to another village to get a shaman to come to Mallango to offer sacrifices, requiring a higher fee for the service because of the extra time involved.

Our last Sunday in Mallango before leaving for a year back home in Australia was memorable for us and also for Ampug. She was baptised. That night she became seriously ill. Everyone thought she was dying, convinced it was because she had turned her back on the spirits and had given up her role as shaman. We had seen enough to believe that was quite possible.

As she became weaker, Ampug's unbelieving relatives pleaded with her to sacrifice a pig so that the spirits would spare her life. She refused, fully aware that she was risking vengeance by the spirits, and instead she called the elders to pray for her.

As they prayed, Ampug had a vision. In it she saw the spirits that had been her constant companions. They were running away from her, terrified. Next morning she was outside laughing and walking around, completely recovered.

In the five villages with which we had the most contact, there were eleven spirit mediums. Within two years of Ampug believing, all but one had accepted the Lord and stopped serving the spirits.

Lìit, a woman about 30 years old, had been a believer for just six months when we gave her a Gospel of John. She started to read it that very night. Next morning she told us that she hadn't been able to put it down until she had finished reading it just after dawn. When we were telling a group of our neighbours about our furlough plans and our concern because we didn't have a place to stay yet, Lìit interrupted us, "The Lord said, 'Look at the birds of the air, and the flowers of the field....' He looks after them. Why can't you trust Him to look after you too?"

We felt privileged to be encouraged by this young Christian—but more than a little ashamed at having to be told by a fairly new believer what we should have known naturally after all our years as Christians.

Just trusting God

"Please, you must come! It's my wife—I think she's dying! Please come and pray for her!"

In Arngikan, twenty minutes' hike south of Mallango, Pinsang was seriously ill. Her husband, Kiyachan, had run to Mallango and was appealing for Saryong and the other elders to go and pray for her.

Saryong, standing on his front porch, listened to Kiyachan's pleas in silence. Although he said not a single word in response, his face clearly exposed an inner turmoil. It was already late afternoon, and even if they hurried, they might not get back home before nightfall.

It was dangerous for Saryong to go outside Mallango, particularly after dark. A clan from Bangad, the village down on the river, had attempted many times to waylay him and kill him in revenge for a murder committed by his cousin some 14 years earlier. Therefore, he seldom left the relative security of his village, even with companions.

Saryong decided he couldn't go; he turned, went back inside his house, and closed the door.

I knew Saryong was struggling—by going he would taking a huge risk. The death threat against him was ever present. Hadn't he already suffered enough distress from his unbelieving fellow villagers who constantly taunted him because of his faith, especially when his own wife wasn't healed while others were? Sure, God had protected him many times already; he

New Experiences

knew that. And yet, he so keenly wanted to live a life of complete obedience to the Lord. Was this to be his time to die?

Kiyachan and Pinsang were new believers, and the infant church in Arngikan needed encouragement. If Pinsang died, Saryong would feel he had failed the believers when they needed him. But was he willing to risk his own life?

Moments later outside Saryong's home, five of the elders assembled outside Saryong's home armed with spears and machetes for security on the trail to Arngikan. They called to Saryong to lead them, but no response came from inside the house. I interpreted his silence as unwillingness to go.

Then the door opened and Saryong emerged, his face showing nothing of the turmoil he must surely have been experiencing. With a calm voice he declared, "I'll go, but I won't carry any weapons!"

Startled by his determination to go, particularly with dusk approaching, I couldn't help appealing to him, "Won't you at least carry a machete?"

"I will just trust God to protect me," he said.

"Then so will I!" one of the others said without hesitation, and all of them discarded their weapons.

I wanted to say, "Don't be foolish!" Instead I asked, "Will you be back before dark?" Saryong assured me they would.

Night came—but they didn't.

At midnight I was still awake, praying and worrying. There had been no sound of shooting or any other commotion from the direction of Arngikan, but that was small comfort to me. The rest of the long night stretched gloomily ahead, and I dozed fretfully.

At dawn they all arrived home, weary but excited. After Saryong and the elders had prayed for Pinsang, the entire village had begged them to stay and talk about their faith, so they had spent the whole night reading from the translated Scriptures and talking about the Lord.

God honoured their obedience to Him. Within weeks all but one in the village of Arngikan had put their trust in Jesus Christ as Saviour.

I hadn't rested that night, but Saryong had—rested and rejoiced, "Just trusting God."

December 1978—time for our furlough year in
Australia: to introduce our two youngest children to our wider family, to renew acquaintances with friends, to report back to our supporters, and to get some rest before returning for what we hoped would be a fruitful second term.

When we arrived home we were thrilled to report to David Cummings. "God has done something beautiful. There are now more baptised believers among the Kalinga church than in our home church!" There were 115 believers altogether, mostly in Mallango.

NINE

Nervous Times

Encouragement to return

While home in Australia in 1979, we
received a dozen letters from friends
in the villages telling of continuing
growth in the church. They made us want
to hurry back to Mallango.

Victoria wrote: "The church is still growing. The chapel is
not big enough for all the people. Many are coming from other
villages. Every Thursday we have two prayer meetings, one
with the men in the morning led by Saryong, and the other
with the women in the evening led by me.

"I appreciate the part the Lord has given me to do in His
work and especially the keenness of the people to learn the
Word of God. Elders are going to Guinaang (the next language
group to the north) to teach and preach the Gospel to the
people there.

"Truly we are missing you and longing for you to hurry
and return to us again."

Palongpong wrote: "We are missing you very much.
We thank God for His love for us in sending you to
bring His good Word here so that our thoughts would
be happy. Great are our thanks to you because of your
love for us, for you came to bring us the Word of God. We are
rejoicing that our chapel is too small for us now because there
are so many who are believing. We are thanking our Father
God for His love for us. God is being praised because the fruits
of what you planted concerning Him are being seen."

Nervous Times

"We are going each week to the other villages, and the number of believers in those places continues to increase.

"Don't be worrying about us whom you left here, for God is caring for us."

Twenty believers, mostly from Mallango, hiked over five hours south to the village of Chananao. They wanted to tell the people there about Jesus. Arriving early in the afternoon, they were soon sharing the Gospel message with curious Chananao people who greeted them. Before long, almost the entire village had gathered to listen.

They talked all that night, all the next day, and the next night as well. The Chananao people wanted to hear everything the believers knew and wouldn't let them stop for sleep. The following morning, the visitors reluctantly decided to leave so they could get some rest. They were exhausted.

As they left the village, people pleaded with them, "Please come back and tell us more."

Because of civil unrest in the area, they weren't able to return for several years. However, God was still working. A man from Chananao who had gone to Bontoc, the main town in a neighbouring language group, started going to a church there, was converted, and went back to his village. Within two weeks he sent a message to the pastor of the Bontoc church. "Please come," he wrote. "There are twelve here wanting to be baptised."

Kilaw, a man in his late 60s, was the first person in Arngikan to believe. Saryong had talked to him several times about God, and Kilaw had listened intently. Then one day, after Saryong had finished sharing with him, he said, "I understand. I have no doubt this is the truth."

Ammoya told us, "As Kilaw began to understand, he and others from Arngikan often came to Mallango to hear God's

154

Word. Then God's Word, the Good News, struck his heart.
Now he is one of the leaders announcing God's Word.
That is a gift from God to Kilaw."

He became so excited about his new faith and the difference that God had made in his life that he went to a nearby
village, Filung, and talked about the Lord to anyone who
would listen. Many believed, and they in turn told others
about the Lord, and within 15 months, 60 of the 75 families
there were believers.

Even though Kilaw can't read, he is recognized as "an expert
at telling what he knows." He's made several trips to Sumachor,
the largest village in Southern Kalinga. Going from house to
house, he talked about God, and soon 30 people were
believing.

Hard times for others

On a beautiful morning in October 1979, Dan Miller
flew to Mallango. His passengers from New Zealand
were going to visit Pam and Rosalie, who with Carol were in
the village teaching literacy at the time. They left Bagabag at
6 a.m. since high cloud cover signaled the approach of bad
weather fuelled by a typhoon approaching the east coast.

Approaching Mallango, Dan observed that the cloudbank
that lay just over the airstrip appeared to be moving away very
slowly. After circling several times he made his approach to
what he described as "landing on a cloud." Perhaps it was the
angled approach combined with the close-by cloud cover, or
the slight breeze coming up the steep mountain alongside the
runway, or the misjudged altitude over the short runway, but
the landing was hard and Dan was concerned. After he taxied
to the top and turned around, he looked under the cowling
and found damage to the structure sufficient to ground the
plane and require someone to come with tools to repair it
before flying out.

Nervous Times

The typhoon hit later that day, and Dan soon realised he wouldn't see another aircraft for some time. Since the New Zealand family needed to catch an international flight in a couple of days, they left the village early next morning, hiking out to catch a series of buses and jeepneys that would take them back to Manila. Dan, however, was destined to stay two weeks longer. He accepted that it would be a while and decided to make the most of it. We were grateful to him when we heard about the many hours he had spent working on the repairs needed to our house.

The daily routine of long visits with the village people started after they had breakfast. The house they were staying in included a *sala* (living room) which was the open visiting room for all who wished to stop by. Since the visitors were a curiosity, many came to use their few words of English, or to speak through an interpreter to learn all they could about them and their families.

One afternoon one of their many visitors lingered until all the others had left. Dan sensed that Saryong wanted to talk with him alone. After several minutes of small talk, Saryong began to tell Dan what was on his heart. He said, "While teaching in another village from the Scriptures that we already have translated, several men from a guerrilla group came in and disrupted the service. They demanded that I quit teaching or they would kill me. After they left, however, I resumed teaching. Several nights later, the guerrillas returned and reminded me about their threat. They swore that if I didn't stop teaching God's Word they would kill my children one by one until I stopped."

He stopped speaking and looked down at the floor. It was hard for Dan to hear what Saryong was telling him. It was even harder when Saryong lifted his head, looked right into Dan's eyes, and slowly and deliberately asked, "What should I do?"

Dan froze. He prayed silently, "Dear Lord, please guide me in my answer." He had never encountered a question like that!

He'd been in the Philippines long enough to appreciate what children mean to a Filipino family.

Believing it was a word from God, Dan looked into Saryong's eyes and said, "I can only remind you of Scriptural examples. God protected Peter and John when they continued to teach after being ordered not to. Paul, on the other hand, fled because of threats on his life. God's Word shows us that we can rely on His Holy Spirit to guide and protect us in everything we do." He prayed with Saryong and encouraged him to trust God to show him when he should teach and when he should be silent. The guerrillas never returned.

The whole year we were in Australia, we couldn't wait to get back to the Philippines. However, within months of arriving back in the Philippines, we couldn't wait to leave! Our first year back was a hard year. It was the year I was almost killed.

A puzzling greeting

On our return to the Philippines in January 1980, there was a message from Palongpong waiting for us. The first part of his letter excited us. "While you have been away," he wrote, "the number of believers has grown. We have nearly doubled in one year, from 115 to 225, and there are churches in five villages." We wanted to go to Mallango right away.

The rest of Palongpong's message was puzzling. He wrote, "You should not come back to Mallango!" He gave no reason.

What did he mean? Just for a short while? Or never again? What was the reason? We wanted to get back and see the New Testament through to completion.

We felt quite downhearted that night and the next day, with our thoughts running out of control. We wished he had written some explanation. What if we couldn't go back to Mallango at all? It was unthinkable. Dave Ohlson, our personnel director at that time, and Jo Shetler both suggested that I go and find out. Since I knew Palongpong wouldn't have written those words lightly, I was a little apprehensive, but I made plans to leave in ten days anyway.

I felt nervous during those ten days and didn't sleep well. On the morning I was to fly to Mallango it was too foggy in Bagabag to take off. The following morning Dan Miller was able to fly out at 6:30 a.m. during a brief break before the fog would have prevented our leaving again.

Within 36 hours I was beginning to wish the fog had stopped us after all!

After landing, I asked the first people I saw if it was safe for me to be there. They all said it was, so I decided to stay.

It was wonderful seeing the believers again. They all welcomed me very warmly and assured me it was safe for me there. Palongpong couldn't be persuaded to tell me why he had sent us the message.

I sat and talked all day with Saryong, Ammoya and others. It was a really wonderful day. Kilaw came from Arngikan and spent most of the day with us too. He showed great excitement as he talked about his faith in the Lord, and he had some very encouraging words for the other believers there in the house with us. I slept very well that night.

I worked with Ammoya all next day, going over some revision needed on the epistles we'd translated before we left for Australia. Domingo also came and helped for a while. Everything seemed fine—until I went outside for coffee at dusk.

While I was chatting with some of the men, a young fellow named Parawag, who had obviously been drinking, walked into the village, stood in front of me and smiled. I smiled back. I opened my mouth to say something pleasant to him, but before I could speak, his smile suddenly changed to a frown and he said, "I'm going to shoot you!"

Fortunately he didn't have his gun with him—it was in his house at the other end of the village. A little shaken and not really comprehending what was being said, I looked straight at him. Then he asked what seemed to me an odd question, "Would you like me to do it now or tonight?"

I felt numb. I didn't know how to respond so I simply replied, "Well, I'd prefer tonight!"

I then remembered seeing Parawag the previous day soon after I had arrived. He had asked me something, but I hadn't understood him. Saryong had responded, but I hadn't understood what he said either. When I asked Saryong about it later, he had told me not to worry about it, so I didn't.

As Parawag and I stood there face to face, no one moved to separate us and no one spoke. All the men there with me, most of them believers, appeared distressed. Saryong was shaking; his fists were clenched, but he kept them by his side. He obviously wanted to stop Parawag, but since they were related he couldn't touch him.

After yelling at me for several minutes, accusing me of being an imperialist and a spy and wanting their land, and telling me I would die, he was successfully persuaded by one of the men to move on. I was relieved.

After the incident, there seemed to be a general feeling of fear among the believers. Saryong and Palongpong advised me to leave the village, "because others might be inspired by Parawag's action." I had no idea what they meant. Then they told me about some of the incidents that had occurred while we had been in Australia.

The leadership of the rebel group had changed during the year, and the new commander and many of his followers had come to Mallango several times. They had called all the villagers together and told them we were imperialists, likening us to the Spaniards who came to the Philippines under the guise of religion and then took over the country.

Nervous Times

He also accused us of being spies for the government, alleging that the president had made a contract with the Australian government to send us to the Philippines to spy on the Kalinga people. He also insisted that the "religion" we had introduced was only a cover for our real purpose of spying, and our reward would be possession of their land.

I couldn't understand how anyone would have believed his story, until Palongpong said, "It's not true, is it?" It was only then that I realised what the believers must have endured while we were away. If an elder of the church, a close friend, had even the slightest doubt about our reason for being there, then they must have suffered much.

When I went to our house that night, two elders came to stay with me. They gave me advice about how to survive the night: "Don't sleep on your bed—they know where that is and will shoot through the wall. Don't stand near the windows—they will see you. If anyone calls out, don't answer, and don't go outside."

We did all the things I guess we're supposed to do in a situation like that—we prayed, sang hymns and read the Scriptures to encourage each other. As midnight approached, I couldn't stay awake any longer, and fell asleep.

About two hours later, Parawag and two of his friends arrived. They stood outside, calling to me, "Bruce, come out here! We're going to kill you!"

For fifteen minutes they called, louder and more impatient as the time passed, but I failed to emerge. Then suddenly, for some reason still unknown to us even now, they stopped calling and left.

But I hadn't heard a thing! I was sound asleep! The elders were awake and praying, but I believe God mercifully kept me sleeping.

Next morning, the elders met to discuss my plight. They decided that I should leave the following day and stay away for at least a month to let things quiet down. They wanted to stay that day for fellowship that night.

I didn't feel confident at all about staying the extra day, but agreed. I sat and talked with some men in Saryong's house for most of the day.

Saryong told me that while we'd been away in 1979, he had stopped teaching in the church and even left Mallango for a while. His main reason for doing that was the criticism he received for teaching on tithing, where believers give a tenth of their income to God's work.

He asked me what should be done about the believers who refuse to tithe. I suggested he not say anything more about it to them for now, and when they were ready to do it, they would be the ones to bring up the subject. But Saryong and Palongpong disagreed with me, and said they must continue teaching it because "a Christian is not obedient if he is not tithing—it's a vital part of their growth and obedience."

Saryong said that the church must have offerings so there would be help available for those who badly needed it. The money from the sale of the widow Amay's coffee trees was almost gone, and she had nothing left to sell in order to buy food for her family. Saryong felt that the church should give her enough money to enable her to start a garden. Also, when the believers in Filung were ready to begin building their chapel, the Mallango believers wanted to be able to help them with finances. Plus, the Mallango chapel, still not completed, already needed extending to accommodate the increasing numbers attending services.

Saryong testified that before he tithed, he never seemed to have enough money; but when he started tithing, contrary to natural expectations, he found that he always had enough money left for his family's needs. His face was beaming as he said that.

His expression became more serious as he told of other events that had occurred while we were away. Some people in the village—he described them as a "faction" who were jealous of Saryong because of his role in the church—tried to discredit him and thus destroy his ministry. They had teenage boys watching him from the time he went outside his house in the morning until he went inside again at night, looking for a chance to accuse him of any wrongdoing. When he taught in the church on Sundays, they tried to distract him by calling out insults and attempting to belittle him and his message.

They also tried to upset Palongpong and Ammoya. Once when Ammoya was teaching, he was so disturbed by their words that he abruptly stopped talking and walked out of the building. He was concerned that he might sin by saying something bad in response to their ridicule and what he was teaching about God.

Saryong eventually found the strain so great that he stopped teaching in Mallango and instead went to teach in other villages. Within a month his insulters back in Mallango, who kept going to services so they could disrupt them, complained to Saryong. They said, "We are getting nothing from the Mallango services, and it seems we only come to yawn!" They wanted Saryong to return to teaching in Mallango. He was reluctant to do that because he knew what was really in their minds.

One day all the elders and deacons went to see Saryong together. They pleaded with him to return to Mallango because he was their best teacher. He agreed, reluctantly. After his first service back in Mallango, the instigator of the plot to discredit him walked past his house that afternoon, carrying a spear and a well-sharpened machete. Fearing the man planned to kill him, Saryong asked his wife to pray with him. The man didn't return.

During the funeral gathering for Lakinchay, Tillao, a deacon in the church, drank too much wine. The following day his daughter Tona became ill. She was soon so weak that her family decided to take her to the Tinglayan hospital. While she was sitting on her hospital bed, she had a vision. She saw two roads, one wide and the other narrow. The wide road went straight ahead, while the narrow road went up and away to the right.

In her vision, when she tried to walk on the wide road, she found it was covered with sharp stones which hurt her feet. When the pain became too much to bear, she looked up and saw a large open book above it. It seemed to be pointing her in the direction of the narrow road. She decided to walk on the narrow road instead, and the moment she stepped onto it, she became well.

As she described the vision later to her father, Tillao realised there was a message in it for him. He had gone the wrong way by getting drunk, and he needed to get back onto the narrow road, God's road, and obey Him. He picked up the Scripture translation that lay near him and opened it. It was First Timothy, and it fell open at the third chapter. The first words his eyes set on referred to one of the qualifications for being a deacon in the church (verse 8): "Deacons must be people who are respected and have integrity. They must not be heavy drinkers..." (NLT).

It would be a long time before he tasted liquor again.

It was good, though sometimes hard, hearing their stories. God was helping them to grow. Although it was often with pain, they were grateful for His care of them.

Meanwhile, after the evening meal on my second nervous night in Mallango, Saryong called the elders and deacons for a Bible study. Several other people also came.

There were three prayer requests on behalf of believers who were sick, including Lùfay, Saryong's wife. Saryong delegated three people to pray for each of the needs. They were nervous, but agreed. Chappay prayed first, then Os-ag, then Chassay.

Nervous Times

That was the first time Chassay had prayed in public. Their prayers were very moving—they prayed like they had been strong Christians for 20 or 30 years.

Saryong wanted me to give a study, and although I was still reluctant to take any part that might make me look like a leader, I felt I should agree to his request this time. At last I had an opportunity to present the study I had prepared on elders and deacons some 18 months before.

I dug out all I could from Titus 1:6–9, and it took me about 30 minutes. Then I asked Saryong if he had anything to add. He spoke for another 45 minutes, and I felt privileged hearing him teach. I was so enthralled that I forgot the danger I was still in. After Saryong finished, he and Awingan prayed for the believers and also for me. I appreciated their concern and care.

Saryong and Palongpong decided to stay with me again that night, and we chatted until nearly midnight when we decided it was time to sleep. They had no trouble sleeping, as usual, but I tossed and turned all night.

Next morning the weather was fine. The plane would have no trouble landing, as long as it arrived before the wind changed from northerly to southerly. Only Saryong and Palongpong knew it was coming, and they told no one until it was nearly at Mallango.

Even with the threat hovering over me, I found it hard to leave Mallango, and it was with a heavy heart that I shook hands with the few elders who accompanied me to the airstrip. I was fearful for their safety and feeling like I was running away from them and leaving them to face many unknowns. They didn't seem concerned, however, and they promised to let us know when it was safe for us to return.

At least once a month the believers from the other villages all came to Mallango for what they called "general assembly." They were planning the next assembly for the following Sunday, and it would have been great to stay for that. I'm sure it would have been a wonderful experience, with probably 250 there for worship and Bible study. Since few of the believers in Filung had been baptised, there was to be a baptismal service too, with perhaps 80 being baptised. It was hard to leave and miss that experience.

Against better judgment

Three months after leaving Mallango there was still no word that it was safe to return. We tried being patient, but found it too difficult. What was happening? Eager to be back with the people, we decided that rather than continue to wait for word from the elders that it was safe to return, we'd fly there and take a look.

We sent a radio message to the Mallango elders through the Catholic mission in a nearby language group, telling them that we were planning to fly there on May 12 and that we would know it was safe for us to land if the windsock was in place; if it wasn't safe, they should not put it up. On May 12 we took off from Bagabag at dawn, with pilot Dan Miller, and headed north to Mallango.

As we crossed the last ridge and the village came into view, we were disappointed to see there was no windsock at the airstrip.

We circled the village and the airstrip for about fifteen minutes, flying as low as 100 metres above the houses. Dozens of people were running towards the airstrip, waving enthusiastically, almost frantically it seemed to us. There was no doubt in our minds that they were beckoning us to land. Remembering previous problems with wind gusts, Dan wasn't prepared to risk a landing without the windsock in place to help him. We willed him to try landing but knew he wouldn't. Then he broke off circling and headed back towards Bagabag. It was a sad trip back for us.

Next morning we received an urgent radio message from the Mallango elders through the priest at Bagabag: "You must

not return to Mallango until we tell you it's okay to come."
We reluctantly accepted the situation.

Two weeks later Ammoya, Palongpong and Kilin arrived at
Bagabag. They told us that the frantic waving of the people,
which we had interpreted as their enthusiastic welcome, was
not to have us land but to leave the area quickly! Some rebels
were there, including two at the airstrip itself. We were relieved
that they hadn't shot at the plane.

We also learned that the rebel commander had been in
Mallango again, repeating his charges against us. He had said,
"Those missionaries are only here for the purpose of eventually taking over all your land." He had made such accusations
before, and while no one believed him, no one ever risked
contradicting him.

Our three extremely welcome visitors told us that another
49 believers had been baptised in April and May—29 from
Filung, 10 from Man-ofar, 5 from Sumachor and 5 from
Mallango.

When they returned to Mallango a month later, two leaders
of the Balangao church, Doming and Mario, went with them.
They wanted to teach and encourage the believers for a few
days. Doming reported later that there were more at the
Sunday service in Mallango than at the Balangao Bible
Conference.

Safe at last

At the end of July, more than five months after I'd
had to leave Mallango, we received the news we'd waited
so impatiently to hear—it was safe to return to Mallango.
We flew there next morning.

Landing on the airstrip brought a deep sense of relief, not
just because we'd landed safely—our hearts were always in our
mouths as we landed at Mallango—but because we had
returned "home" at last. We'd been able to continue working
on the translation during our enforced absence from the

village, when people came out to help us; but it wasn't as good a work situation as actually being there among the people. We wanted to be immersed in the culture and all the activities of the village.

Ammoya was waiting for us, as we climbed out of the plane. He smiled broadly and called out, "God has answered my prayers!" He added that if we hadn't arrived by the following day he, Marnawa and Saryong would have gone to fetch us.

Then Ammoya filled us in on some of the events in Mallango during our time away. We were disappointed to hear that Udchus had turned away from following the Lord and was actually encouraging those who opposed the believers, by disrupting the prayer meetings. He was often drunk.

Tong-ag, the first believer in Filung and leader of the church there, had also turned away from the Lord. He had shown evidence of growth in his faith when he attended the Balangao Bible Conference at Easter, but two months later he killed a pig that didn't belong to him. Soon after that, he turned away from the Lord and told the believers they were wrong to believe the Bible, "Because it's no use."

Many of the Filung believers were confused by the change in Tong-ag, and some had come to Mallango to ask the elders for help. Ammoya and Palongpong went to a service there one Sunday.

They found opposition. Chawakan, a former village leader in Filung, asked them lots of questions about the Lord, but all of his questions had a twist to them. Whatever they said in answering, he turned it into a criticism of God, the Bible or the believers. He was doing what they called "philosophising." I used to get agitated when people did that, as I felt so helpless, unable to counter their arguments in a way that would stop them. Ammoya and Palongpong were much more patient than me, and instead of getting upset they answered the best they could from the Scriptures and left it at that.

Nervous Times

The following Sunday, they were surprised to see Chawakan come to the service in Mallango. Kinit, the new leader of the church in Filung, told them later that Chawakan was believing now. He had thought through the answers of Ammoya and Palongpong during the week and had come to the realisation that he needed to change and follow their teaching. Palongpong told us that Chawakan was an influential man in Filung and that he would be very helpful in convincing others there of their need to follow the Lord.

On our first Sunday back in Mallango, the morning service went for three hours. Domingo was the preacher. The chapel was packed solid, with dozens also sitting on the ground outside. I estimated there were over 200 present, including people from four other villages. Saryong and I had planned to go to Sumachor that afternoon, but the leader of the believers there, Issì, had sent word that we shouldn't go. We guessed there was a good reason but didn't know what it was.

A number of events occurred during the next couple of weeks, both good and bad. The mayor of Tinglayan, Alngag, was killed by men from the village of Butbut. When his son in Tuguegarao heard about it, he killed a Butbut man in revenge. We were told that in the municipal elections, Alngag had actually been defeated by the Butbut candidate, Bagtang, but Alngag was declared the winner. That caused bad blood between the two villages.

One day, to Emma's surprise, Saryong gave her a Mallango name, the name of his mother, Awanon. That was a beautiful gesture and very special to Emma.

In August, Judith's mother, Doris Fletche, and her friends, Alf and Edna Hooper, arrived to visit us for five days. On our second Sunday back we all hiked to Arngikan for the service there. Several from Mallango, Sumachor and Filung also went. Saryong preached, and he was excellent.

During the service the believers discussed the concept of revenge. There was trouble between two of the villages, and traditionally people would exact revenge on anyone who harmed them. The believers wanted to know how they should react now that they were Christians. After a lot of discussion, without any resolution, Saryong read Hebrews 10:30, "For we know the one who said, 'I will take vengeance. I will repay those who deserve it...'" (NLT).

That settled the matter. There was no more discussion needed. They were satisfied, and they went on with discussion of other matters.

Next morning Mr. Flores Tiggangay, newly appointed Division Supervisor for the Tinglayan and Tanudan schools, unexpectedly arrived in Mallango to visit the school. I took the opportunity to meet him. He was full of praise for SIL because of the tribute that the Tinglayan district had received from the Ministry of Education and Culture for the literacy program in Mallango and its large number of graduates.

When refreshments were brought out, I was asked to pray. When I finished Mr. Tiggangay looked at me with obvious curiosity and asked, "Where did you learn to pray like that?" He had only heard written prayers recited before.

TEN

The Importance of Drinking Coffee

A good day for an execution

Sunday, August 17, 1980. A good day for an execution. My execution! That morning several of us hiked to Filung, southwest of Mallango, in response to an invitation from the leaders of the church there. Twenty-one new believers wanted to be baptised. Several from Mallango were happy to go, and I gladly joined them, keen to see the Filung church in action. Judith and the children didn't come with me this time. That was fortunate, as it turned out.

It took 20 minutes to reach Arngikan, where Kilaw joined us for the 50-minute hike further on to Filung. It was a difficult hike—at least for me, not used to hiking over steep hills and along narrow rice terraces. I followed Kilaw, careful to put my feet where his had been before me. I remember gazing at his aged, wrinkled feet as they cautiously negotiated the winding, stony path. They reminded me of Isaiah 52:7, "How beautiful on the mountains are the feet of those who bring good news of peace and salvation..." (NLT).

When the believers from Mallango and Arngikan heard that the brook selected for the baptisms was between Filung and the next village, they refused to go any further. There was tribal warfare between the two villages, and going out to the brook would literally put them in the firing line.

In response to this danger, the Filung elders decided to use the spring that trickled through the village. This meant they

171

The Importance of Drinking Coffee

would first need to dig a hole large enough for two people, the one doing the baptising and the one being baptised, to stand in comfortably, and it would take some time for the water to become clear.

There were about 50 adults at the service, which was held in the school building just outside the village. It went for three hours and included teaching by Kinit and others on baptism. The sermon took up most of the service time. I wasn't asked to participate at all, but I didn't mind. It was exciting watching them do everything themselves.

One of the men in Filung expressed his gratitude to us. "We thank God," he said, "for putting it in your mind to translate the Bible into our language. Now that we have the Word of God, we here in Filung know that it is true, for we can read it ourselves. Even we who didn't go to school can understand. People here would not be believing if you had not obeyed what God commanded you to do."

Kinit, who was leading the group of believers in Filung, said, "During my childhood, I learned to do all the customs my parents observed. There was nothing that we didn't obey of the customs handed down to us by our ancestors. But when I grew up, I obeyed nothing and no one, except myself. I did whatever I wanted to do. If someone gave good advice, or tried to stop me from doing bad things, I refused to listen to him.

"When the Gospel came to our place, I could see the changes in those who believed it. When I said bad words to them, they only said good words back to me; when I said the opposite of what God's Word says, they persisted in speaking the truth.

"I began to ask the believers questions, and their answers were good. I kept asking questions of those who were teaching God's Word, and I listened to what they said and what they read from God's Word in our own language as I began to believe."

The Importance of Drinking Coffee

"I went to church services so I could hear more of God's Word, but I sat off to one side. I wanted to just observe what was said and done in the church, without being conspicuous. After one month, I understood what God wants to tell us.

"Then I started to read His Word myself. Now it's as if I have an insatiable thirst to read it. I am very happy because God's Word is now hidden in my mind.

"When the foreigners first came, we thought they were spies and would sell us (betray us). We thought they planned to trick us and somehow take our land. Then we began to understand that was all untrue. We discovered that they were here to bring God's Word to us, and it was because they understood God's Word themselves that they wanted to bring it to us."

Another man, Amrus, testified, "When the Espiritistas (Spiritualists) came here, I was the first one to be convinced to follow their teachings. Many others joined us too. But when our leader died, most of the people stopped meeting with us.

"Then, one day I was walking along the trail and I saw the old man Sìchawag. He was reading a book and I asked him what it was. He told me it was part of the Bible (God's Word to people) that had been translated into his own language, and it is.

"I asked him what time the people in Mallango gathered together to study and he said, 'Every Sunday morning.' When Sunday came, I went with Apingaw to Mallango to hear God's Word. After that I often went to listen, and the time came that I believed. Now it's natural for me to crave God's Word.

"If this Word of God had come earlier, I would have believed earlier. I would not have had to sell all our possessions because of our customs regarding the spirits, which demand animals to be sacrificed. Many have now put aside the customs that Satan wants us to follow. Truly, many more will turn to God as His Word is proclaimed."

The Importance of Drinking Coffee

The baptisms were to take place after the service, but someone reported that the water was still muddy so we decided to have lunch first.

As we entered the village, someone called out, "The meat's not cooked yet. Come and have some coffee while you're waiting." Kilaw, Palongpong and I readily accepted. Everyone was brought a mug of steaming, black, sweet coffee, except me. I was handed mine in a bowl. They knew I loved coffee.

After we'd drunk our fill, we set off again for the house where we would eat, but again we were stopped. "The meat's still not cooked," reported a helpful neighbour. "Come and have some more coffee." Since I never refused coffee, we accepted his invitation.

Just as we finished drinking, we heard people shouting and crying outside. We looked out and saw women and children running past the house, their mouths wide open in terror. The only time I'd seen people like that before was when Iminya had been controlled by a spirit. Since I'd discovered that casting out evil spirits was not one of my gifts, I decided to stay right where I was.

A few minutes later, Tong-ag came and sat on the porch. His face and actions gave no hint of anything wrong, but I asked him anyway, "What's happening, brother?" He didn't answer. The other men with me also asked but got the same stony response.

Curious, Kilaw decided to go and look for himself. A few seconds later, I heard him shouting, "If that's what you want, bring him out and kill him here in front of everyone, but you'll have to kill me too!"

Kill Kilaw? And who else? Who was he talking to? I hadn't heard anyone talk to spirits that way before, but my curiosity wasn't strong enough to get me outside to see better. I was happy to stay right where I was.

174

A few minutes later Kilaw came back, whispered something to Palongpong, then went again. There was still a tremendous commotion going on. Three times Kilaw came back, and finally I asked Palongpong, "What's going on?"

He didn't answer, but he was shaking. After I asked him a third time, he replied, with obvious reluctance, "There are two men with guns, and they want to shoot someone!"

"Who?" I asked.

"You!" he answered.

He directed me to go and sit in the darkest corner of the house, then he said, "Let's pray."

I had been doing well until that moment, but as soon as he said those words, a cold wave of fear suddenly shot through me. Whoever, or whatever, was outside was going to kill me.

The moment Palongpong started praying, the fear instantly left me. He only said a few words, however, and then stopped. I could see he was distressed. All I can remember uttering was a barely audible, shaky, "Please help us, Lord!" Palongpong then told me that Abfù and Lamfayung, members of the rebel group, had been drinking, become drunk, and decided it was time to get rid of me. They were going from house to house searching for me to kill me.

As the yelling and crying continued outside, Kilaw came in and said firmly, "We must leave now."

As I moved clumsily towards the doorway, the owner of the house, who had been sitting near the fireplace, spoke for the first time since the incident had begun. "Oh, don't go," he said matter-of-factly. "We haven't eaten yet."

Kilaw threw up his hands, mumbled something that wasn't clear to me, pointed towards me and ordered, "Outside! Now!" I glanced at our host, shrugged my shoulders, and walked quickly outside.

I left the village quickly, flanked by several men. Abfù and Lamfayung were just a couple of houses away from us by that time, calling my name. Some of the believers blocked their path to give us a chance to escape. Women alongside the trail were crying, and saying, "No! It can't be! You came here for a good purpose, and they are doing this. This should not be happening."

As we stumbled along the trail, I said nothing. I couldn't find any words to say. I couldn't believe this was happening. Mark 13:14–17 came to my mind as I listened to Kilaw, Palongpong and Kinit talking. They were discussing how they expected persecution to become worse. "We can expect persecution because that's what it says in the Scriptures," Kilaw said, "but we know God will be with us. If we are killed, God will raise up even stronger leaders to replace us. And even if some believers fall away from their faith because of the hardship they will suffer, the faith of others will grow."

Reaching Arngikan in 45 minutes, we stopped for an hour at Kilaw's house to drink coffee and eat while waiting for the others from Mallango to catch up. I wasn't hungry. I did, however, drink a large amount of coffee.

When Ammoya arrived, he told us he had been sitting outside the house where we were to eat in Filung, when Abfù and Lamfayung appeared. They told him to call me outside so they could shoot me. Ammoya told them I wasn't there, but they insisted he go inside and bring me out. When he refused to move, Lamfayung went inside. When they saw I wasn't there, they started looking in other houses. Ammoya said he was afraid at first, but after he prayed his fear was removed.

When we reached Mallango, I joined the elders in Palongpong's house to discuss the situation. Their conclusion was that we should leave Mallango until the situation improved.

I didn't tell Judith much about the incident in Filung, for several reasons—it was hard to get the words out; I didn't want to upset her; and I was confused. Relieved that she and the children had not gone to Filung with me that day, I simply told her that we were home earlier than expected because of "some trouble." I tried to think that somehow this problem would pass like the previous one eventually had, and that it would be easy to talk about it another day.

We decided to leave next morning, but the elders asked us to stay another day. They wanted to have some fellowship with us on the Monday night.

Saryong particularly wanted us to stay the extra day. "It might be the last time you will see me alive!" he said. He wouldn't explain what was behind that statement.

Another day, another attempt on my life

At daybreak on Monday, I went to Palongpong's house for coffee and to firm up our plans for the following day. Saryong joined us. He hadn't been in Filung with us and was extremely upset about what had happened. He had been discussing our plight with some of the believers in Mallango, and they had all agreed that we should leave for a while.

Palongpong offered to come to Bagabag after six weeks if it was still not safe to return to Mallango by then. Saryong said we shouldn't even think about returning until the elders decided it was definitely safe for us there. I called Bagabag and requested a flight for Tuesday morning.

Around 9 a.m. on Monday, Ammoya and Palongpong came and sat in our kitchen. They didn't want to talk; they just wanted to sit. Later, Issì arrived from Sumachor. He told us that after my escape the previous day, Abfù and Lamfayung had gone to Sumachor to enlist others to accompany them to Mallango that night. They were planning another attempt to kill me. Issì became angry, and drove them from his village, telling them they weren't welcome there, so they went back to Filung.

As Issì left us, tears in his eyes, he said simply, "Please don't forget the believers." We didn't understand why he would say that.

The Importance of Drinking Coffee

Soon after, I began to feel unsettled, and at 10.30 a.m. I asked Ammoya and Palongpong if they still felt it was okay for us to wait till the next day to leave. Without hesitation they said there was no danger that day. The same question from me at 11 a.m. elicited the same response.

By 11.30 a.m., the feeling that something was wrong had become so intense that I shared my uneasiness with Ammoya and Palongpong. This time they said that if God was telling us to leave, then we should obey Him.

I called the SIL Centre, praying that Marge, the radio operator, would still have the radio turned on. Normally she didn't have it on at that time of day because a Chinese broadcast on a frequency close to the one we used was so loud that no one using our frequency could be understood. Since it was impossible to talk above it, Marge usually switched the radio off. We prayed that she would not only have the radio on, but that she would be able to pick up my voice as I tried to attract her attention through the noise.

When I turned the radio on, we were amazed to hear no Chinese. Instead we heard the voice of Jo Shetler. For some reason, Jo had arranged earlier to speak to Marge at that particular time, aware they would have to yell to be heard over the Chinese program, but they were able to speak normally after all. I interrupted them between sentences and asked Marge if I could speak to her urgently. I said, "Since there's no really pressing need for us to stay here till tomorrow, we might as well leave today. Would you mind asking Eric if he could come and pick us up in the helicopter at around 3 o'clock?" I must have sounded a good deal calmer than I felt because Marge suspected nothing.

When Eric received our message, however, he sensed that something was wrong. Back again, with Jo patiently waiting to resume her conversation, Marge told us, "Eric said he'll be there at 1 o'clock."

The Importance of Drinking Coffee

With a lot to be done before we could leave—giving food away, securing the house, saying goodbye to friends—I said, "I doubt we can be ready that quickly. Would you ask him if he could make it 1:30?"

While Marge was away telling Eric, Palongpong burst into the room. He was shaking. Stumbling over his words, he said, "A man has run here from Filung to say that the two trouble-makers are planning to come here some time today for another attempt to kill you. You must leave immediately, and not from the airstrip but from the school ground, because they will be coming from the direction of the airstrip."

Fear suddenly surged through my body again, just like my experience the previous day in Filung.

Marge returned and reported: "Eric will be there at 1:30."

My voice sounded calm, but inside I wasn't feeling at all calm. I said, "Could you ask him to make it 1 o'clock?" It was already noon.

Eric took off minutes later. When I called him to ask how much cargo we could take, he said that since we had to leave from the school ground the helicopter could handle little more than our body weights. He explained that unlike helicopters in the movies, most can't rise straight up. The tall coffee trees that ringed the school ground meant the helicopter would have difficulty lifting off even with just our weight...particularly mine. (Thanks, friend!)

In the 45 minutes we had before the chopper arrived, we secured the house and gave all our food away. Saryong, Palongpong and Ammoya went ahead to the school ground to make sure it was clear while Chappay stayed at the house to help us.

We didn't tell our children why we were leaving so suddenly. It didn't seem unusual to them that we were making such a spur-of-the-moment trip, but David told us later that he had sensed his Mum and Dad were worried and noticed that the people in our house weren't saying anything. Then

The Importance of Drinking Coffee

one of his friends told him there were some people after his Dad. He said his heart sank hearing that news and he became concerned as well. He tried to do exactly what we told him to do, "to try and help reduce the level of tension."

As we walked quickly down to the school, several of the believers accompanied us, surrounding us like the wings of a mother hen shielding her chicks from harm. They were willing to protect us, even at the risk of their own lives. Everyone was upset about what was happening, and many were crying. One said, "We're so sorry you have to leave, but you'll be back soon. Maybe it will only be two months this time, not six like last time." Others nodded in agreement. We nodded in hope.

One of the elders said, "If you want to stay, we will protect you. It's up to you." We knew someone could get hurt, perhaps even killed, and we didn't want that to happen.

With Abfù and Lamfayung reportedly only 15 minutes away from Mallango, the helicopter arrived and cautiously landed in the school ground.

Just then, we were thankful to God for many reasons: for the availability of the helicopter—if it hadn't been there we couldn't have left that day and we don't know what might have happened; for Eric's perceptiveness; for Marge who still had the radio on when it was usually way too distracting at that time of day; and for Jo who had provided the reason for the radio being on.

We were also thankful that none of our language material had to be left behind. When Judith's mother and her friends had left just four days before to do some sightseeing before we joined them later, the helicopter wasn't fully loaded. We decided to fill the cargo space with the language material we weren't using. It just seemed like a good idea at the time. We didn't know what we'd need during the month we planned to be away from Mallango.

As it turned out, our language material would have been too heavy to take with us and we would have had to leave it

180

behind. All we were allowed to take were a change of clothes and the small amount of translation material we were currently working on. David felt sad having to leave a large cardboard castle he had recently made, but he would be able to get it when we returned.

I asked Eric if he would be willing to take one extra item— a bundle of egg cartons. We'd been saving them to return to the lady at Bagabag who bought supplies for people like us out in the mountains. He glanced at the egg cartons, looked at me, and burst into laughter. I felt a little bit silly when I realised what I was asking, but I tried to explain: "These egg cartons are important to her. She's always running short of them." Eric gently relieved me of the cartons and without another word put them under one of the seats.

With our family of six buckled into the four passenger seats available, we were ready to commence our ascent. The next couple of minutes were reminiscent of a wild ride at an amusement park. After a longer than normal warm-up, the chopper lifted slightly and hovered, then lightly rested back on the ground again. It lifted again, swung backwards and for- wards several times until the tail was so high that we looked straight down and felt like we were going to fly straight into the ground. Then, when Eric felt we were high enough to clear the trees, suddenly the engine roared and we swooped down- wards like a roller coaster, dipped to the right, lifted sharply upwards, cleared the trees by at least a metre, and were away.

A hundred thoughts crowded into our minds as we flew away from Mallango; there were many questions, but no answers. Would the believers think we were deserting them? What would happen to them? Would they be discouraged seeing us leave them like this? Should we have stayed? Some would certainly have been hurt trying to protect us. We were doing the only wise thing to do.

We prayed God would care for them. I couldn't see through my tears for most of the flight to Bagabag. Judith and I looked at each other, and tried to talk about the situation, but it was too hard. Our main consolation, apart from the obvious one that we had been able to escape unharmed, was that we would return to Mallango again, hopefully soon. It would have been much harder if we'd known we might not.

It was only when we landed at Bagabag that we told our children the reason we had left Mallango. A few days later, feeling very flat, we wrote to a dear friend in Australia, Olive, to tell her how devastated we were feeling. She wrote back to us, saying, "Remember it's the Lord's work, not yours."

"It's the Lord's work, not ours!" That became our motto for the rest of our time in the Philippines. We kept working on the translation, and the church kept growing and spreading.

Conflict and relief

We had confidence in the fact that God knew more about what was happening, or going to happen, than we did. It was a long while before we began to accept that we might never return to Mallango. We still find it hard, years after leaving, accepting that we had to leave the way we did. During the next two years, I threw myself into the translation in an attempt to take my mind off "things," doing my best to stifle the longing to get right away—to go home to Australia. Otherwise, what happened to me—and what nearly happened—tended to consume my thoughts.

I knew God had called us there, but I didn't want to stay. I wanted to do God's will, and see the translation completed. I tried not to feel that Australia was my only alternative and that God would protect us if we stayed, but still it was hard. My heart knew what we should do, of course, but my head took a lot more convincing.

I felt nervous much of the time and had recurring nightmares—it was a different scenario each time, but with the common theme of someone chasing me, intent on killing me.

The Importance of Drinking Coffee

I was thankful that Judith and the children were happy, and that they felt peace about staying in the country. I was quite successful in hiding my own feelings, but I couldn't imagine carrying such a burden for too many years, or even months.

Two years after the incident, four people had a special prayer time for me—Judith, David and Ruth Cummings, and dear old Sadie Sieker, known to everyone in the organization as Aunt Sadie. I had no more nightmares after that and was happy to stay and complete the translation.

What next?

Six weeks after leaving Mallango, we received a letter from the church elders. They wrote, "You should not return at the present time. When the climate has improved, we will let you know." We guessed the writer wasn't referring to the weather.

It was unsettling not knowing what was happening there, and although we felt uneasy about going back, it hit us hard being told we shouldn't go. We didn't even know if anyone would come out to work with us in Bagabag.

Four days later, Ammoya and Domingo arrived to help us work on the translation. They told us that two days after we left Mallango, the commander of the rebel group arrived to "investigate" the incident. He interviewed Ammoya, Palongpong, Saryong and our landlord George Liban. He wanted to know what had happened in Filung, and why we had left Mallango.

They told him, and he then went to Filung to see Abfù and Lamfayung, the two who had tried to kill me. He later told Ammoya that he hated foreigners and didn't want us there, and that if I went back he would kill me. He repeated his threat on several other occasions too. The only consolation we felt was knowing that although he could stop us working there, he couldn't stop God working.

The Importance of Drinking Coffee

When I asked Ammoya if he thought it would be okay for us to return to Mallango for an hour or two to encourage the believers, he didn't answer. I asked him again, in three different ways, and finally he responded. He said, "My brother, I know you and your family really do want to go back to continue your work, and the believers need you there to encourage them. But you should not go near the place because the rebels are watching for you, and if an 'accident' were to happen, many of the believers would be discouraged." We understood what he was trying to say.

Our landlord sent word with them that we should advise him what to do with our belongings, but we were reluctant to say anything yet because we didn't want to give up our hope of eventually returning. I wrote and asked him to leave things as they were for the time being, and that if anyone should ask him what our "real purpose" was in being there, to tell them we had only one purpose, and that concerned the Gospel, the Good News about Jesus Christ.

Ammoya and Domingo worked hard the first four days, finishing the chapters of Acts that needed revision. During the next four days we translated chapters 13–14. The following morning, Domingo announced that he wanted to return to Mallango soon. He said Ammoya could stay and work with me, but later that day Ammoya said he also needed to go home. Although they had originally assured us they would stay as long as we needed them, they suddenly wanted to leave early.

We never did find out why. Maybe we had worked them too hard. More likely they were concerned about the safety of their families, since word may have reached the rebels that they were helping us.

As that day passed, we could see their minds weren't really on the work, so we said good-bye to them the following morning. Ammoya said he and Palongpong would return to Bagabag ten days later.

The Importance of Drinking Coffee

Two weeks after Ammoya and Domingo left, Udchus and Palongpong arrived. They reported the situation in Mallango unchanged, as far as we were concerned. As we translated Acts 20, where Paul told the elders in Miletus that he was going to leave and they wouldn't see him again, Udchus told us that when we left Mallango everyone was crying. Many wanted to tell us how they were feeling, but they couldn't express themselves in words.

Palongpong said, "There was no joy there at that time." Udchus added, "Every time I think about what happened, and why you had to leave, tears come to my eyes." We all had to stop and wipe our eyes before continuing our work.

A letter from Domingo said, "The rebels have questioned the elders further about what you were doing in Mallango, so we have decided to tell you not to come back because you are really hated by those people."

Udchus then shared some of the reasons for his unusual behaviour back when he first believed. He told us: "After the workshop when I first believed in the Lord, I went home keen to share my joy with my friends. They weren't interested to listen to me, and after a while I found myself turning away from God and instead doing what pleased me. I went back to my old ways. Even when I tried to do good, I couldn't because of the influence of my unbelieving friends.

"The next time you went to a workshop at Bagabag, I decided to go again, hoping that my weakened faith would be strengthened there. My faith did return to some degree. When I returned home that time, my little faith remained but I hid it from others because I knew there were many who would try to discourage me.

"However, I wasn't satisfied doing that, and after a while it came to my mind to ask myself, 'Why am I hiding my faith?' I began to meet with the other believers, and my faith grew strong."

The Importance of Drinking Coffee

"Then I married Lydia, but no one in her family, including Lydia, believed in Jesus. I tried to tell them about Him, but they refused to listen. My wife loved me but I was hated by my in-laws. They caused me many problems. I didn't know what to do about them, so I thought it best to divorce my wife.

"Then I remembered that God had said in His Word that if I divorced my wife I would be sinning against Him. That strengthened my mind. I paid no attention to the harsh words of my in-laws. Instead I paid attention to the Word of God, and I received great encouragement from the other believers so that I no longer turned away from God and His Word.

"Once when my little family experienced a particular hardship, I was extremely upset and didn't know what to do. I didn't think my in-laws would help us. When I reached the end of my tether, I prayed to God. He was my only hope. I asked Him to help us overcome our hardship.

"And He did! Our troubles ended, and my in-laws were amazed. They knew I had not been able to do anything on my own, and that I had handed my problem over to God. I was encouraged when I recalled that God had said in His Word that He would never forsake His people; He would help them in their hardships.

"My faith is strong now. Whatever happens, I don't worry. My obedience to the Lord includes teaching His Word, although sometimes I'm discouraged when someone says, 'You should first teach it to your own household.'

"What encourages me most to want to teach God's Word is what I observe about many people. They understand very little, so I want to share what I have learned as I've been helping to translate the Word of God.

"There have been times when I've tried to escape from His Word, but He wouldn't let me. He has always brought me back to His Word. I have experienced that it's only when I'm obedient that I have peace."

186

"I will try to serve the Lord the way He wants me to, with all my strength."

Three weeks after arriving, Udchus and Palongpong wanted to return to Mallango. Working more than twelve hours a day, we had finished translating Acts, and Reg Giesbrecht, head of our publications department, printed four copies of Acts from the computer, as well as our draft of *Pilgrim's Progress*, for the men to take with them.

Watching their bus disappear in the distance, it suddenly hit me that the translation work was becoming an obsession. I was working day and night and giving very little time to my family. I wanted to see the translation finished before the end of this term on the field, but I was finding little joy in the work.

Translating the Bible should surely be the greatest thrill and pleasure there is, but it had become a burden. I was not able to relax, or spend profitable time with Judith and our children. I realised I had to change, or I would regret it, and my family and our work would all suffer. I'm thankful to God that I was able to change, and spend more time with my family. It meant slowing down the translation work a little but we got the job done anyway.

More encouragement; more discouragement

Christmas 1981 came, and we still hadn't spent a Christmas in the village. We had originally planned several village Christmases in our second term, but now that idea seemed impossible. We didn't know if we'd get back to Mallango at all, let alone for a Christmas.

We expected Udchus and Ammoya to arrive at Bagabag in early January, but the night before they planned to leave Mallango, some rebels had arrived in the village so they decided to wait a while. However, three days later they slipped

The Importance of Drinking Coffee

quietly out of the village without telling anyone except their families and a few of the believers, where they were going.

Old Kilaw sent us a special gift with them. He had walked from his village to Mallango at 2 a.m. the morning they were to leave, just to send us some coffee. We felt greatly loved.

Kilaw also sent us a letter, which he had Saryong write: "Our brother and sister in Christ, we, your fellow believers here in Arngikan, are grateful to our Father God for sending you here to our place in order that we might rejoice through our having faith in Jesus Christ. And we thank you because of the Word you came to plant in us in Arngikan, so that we would understand God's Word and live in Him. We believers here are of one mind and we are happy because of Him.

"When elders first came from Mallango to teach God's Word in our village, I really despised them and I asked them how much they were being paid to teach it. But now I understand God's Word, and I know that the joy they have through serving Jesus Christ is the only reward they want.

"Before I believed, I followed all the customs that had been taught from generation to generation, including the chapilang, the barking of dogs and the sound of pigs. I also followed the ancestral custom regarding killing, and if I wanted to kill a man I could easily do it. When I befriended evil spirits, we would butcher animals to please them.

"Then one day when I heard the Word of God being read and explained, I realised that the work of Satan is not good, but God's work is good. So I gave my body to God, and now I only like to do His work. I know that God has chosen me to preach His Word to my own people, and I love to do that.

"Before I believed, if someone said anything bad to me I would respond worse. But now that I believe in God, I can just swallow any bad things that are said to me. I cannot speak bad back to them. I only want to speak God's words now.

"If only this Good News had come earlier, I would not have had to kill so many animals asked for by the spirits."

The Importance of Drinking Coffee

"I cry for those who cannot understand what God wants to tell them. I pray for my people, that they will understand like I do.

"Great are our thanks to God regarding what happened to us in Filung when Bruce was nearly killed. Since that time our faith has been strengthened. Bruce and Judith, don't worry about us in whom you planted the Word, because it's God we depend on now and we only follow the words of Jesus Christ. Even though I am persecuted, as long as I can teach God's Word I will not be discouraged.

"In our village we are all singing and talking about God's Word. Even though life is still hard, we are happy because God's Word assures us. We thank God for sending Jesus Christ here to show us the truth.

"You should be happy for the believers are growing, especially the old ones, men and women alike. Even though we don't understand everything yet, we insist on believing because we know that although we have no power, God is powerful, and we are praising Him. We know that Jesus Christ is the owner of our minds.

"We are praying for you. We have missed you since you left us, and we are continually praying that some day God will allow us to see you again."

Since the situation was still the same and looked like it would remain that way for a long time to come, I asked Udchus and Ammoya whether the believers would be discouraged if we had some of our belongings brought out. They said they wouldn't be because they knew we were away only because certain people were preventing us from being there.

I was still struggling to accept our situation. I even felt unsafe in Bagabag, but I wanted desperately to see the translation completed.

The Importance of Drinking Coffee

Udchus and Ammoya stayed for a month. A week after they returned home, Udchus and Kinit arrived with some of our possessions. They also brought sad news, and all these years later I still weep when I remember the details.

Udchus reported, "There has been a measles epidemic in our area, and many children have died." He hesitated, then continued, "I'm sorry, my friend, but I have to tell you that your little friend Afay was one of them." I burst into tears, and Udchus hugged me and cried with me. Afay was one of the two little children in Mallango who were never too shy to talk to me or hold my hand. Ambet was the other. Now both my little friends were dead.

Twelve children had died in Mallango, and thirty in Filung, including both of Tong-ag's children and all three of Chongaop's. Tong-ag and his wife had turned away from the Lord. We tried to understand what they had gone through but knew we really couldn't. However, something beautiful happened a few months later. One of the believers, trying to help them, said, "One day you will see your children again in heaven." The Lord used that to restore their faith.

Fanilag and his wife also lost two children. Fanilag wrote to tell us: "I am one who liked to obey God's Word ever since I believed it, and my faith became strong through doing that. In the measles epidemic, my children, Peter and Chawakon, died. Before he died, Peter, who was just six years old, spoke to me. He said, 'Father, let us go to God. I want to be with God, for He is the One who made me, and it's where He is that the best life is. Now I will leave you, and I will go to be with God. He is our only Father. Will you join me there some day?'

"Then he died. We said to ourselves, 'It's true, God called him.' Because of our faith, we have the hope that we will see our children again. Before we knew God, it was very hard for us when our children died, but how different it is now that we believe in God."

The Importance of Drinking Coffee

Changkop wrote, "When the measles epidemic hit our village, three of our four children died, two one day and the third four days later. Our parents and other relatives and some unbelievers said to my wife and me, 'It's obvious that this Word of God that you are studying is not good!'

"They mocked us like that, and they also said other things that were very hard for us to hear, such as, 'This has happened because you changed your religion.'

"We were not discouraged by them because we knew that the Word of God says that we can know that we have faith when we are insulted and persecuted.

"That's how it is with us believers in Filung. All the bad things that must happen to Christians have happened to us. We have been persecuted, insulted, mocked and hated, but these things don't discourage us. Instead, they serve to encourage us in our faith."

Many of the other believers had become discouraged, and we wanted desperately to return there to help them somehow, but we knew it wasn't possible.

There was some unexpected news too—Lamfayung, one of the men who had tried to kill me in Filung, had stopped persecuting the believers.

Lamfayung's seven-year-old son had become very ill during the previous month. He cried day and night from pain. No one knew what was wrong with him, but instead of taking him to a hospital, his family offered sacrifices to the spirits, and even after they had killed all their animals, there was no change in the boy's condition. Lamfayung was so desperate that he went to see Kinit, the leader of the church in his village, and asked him to pray for the child.

Kinit was sick himself, so he told the other elders to go and pray. They were reluctant to, because Lamfayung had been violently opposed to them and they thought it might be a trick—

they might be ambushed and killed if they went to his house. But Kinit encouraged them to go, saying, "This could be our opportunity to share our faith with him," so they went and prayed for the boy, and he was soon sleeping peacefully, healed.

Lamfayung immediately stopped his opposition to the believers and began to attend the church services. Six months later, he became a believer.

On my visit to the Philippines in 1986 to proofread the New Testament manuscript, I left a small camera and two films with Udchus and asked him to take photos of anything that happened in the church that would encourage us. Twelve months later, we received the exposed films in the mail. We could hardly wait to get them developed and see what was on them. One set showed people receiving and reading the New Testament; the other showed several people being baptised. One of them was Lamfayung!

Ammoya's greatest concern was that the Good News should be shared amongst fellow Kalingas in neighbouring villages. His main ministry on Sundays was teaching in Man-ofar, a village about 20 minutes away around rice terraces and over several hills. Together with another elder, he saw that as his God-given responsibility and he loved to do it.

In 1983, Ammoya had a stroke. The whole of his left side was paralysed. He couldn't speak clearly, and it was several months before he could make himself even partially understood. People laughed at his slurred speech—some from embarrassment, others through sheer vindictiveness.

When he was able to hold a pen, he wrote to us at Bagabag in a scrawl that was barely readable: "My brother and sister, I am grateful to our Father God for this testing of my faith. I am still paralysed, I have malaria, and I have a very bad cough. Even though I suffer a lot, I bear it because the Lord Jesus

Christ also suffered much, and I am confident that He will help me to endure my hardship. I am praying that the Lord will use this testing and suffering to strengthen my faith. I thank the Lord Jesus Christ that though my left hand is paralysed He permits me to write with one hand. Thanks to the Lord, our Saviour.

"My sufferings are really only little compared to what He experienced, but please pray that He will make me well again so that I can resume my responsibility of going to teach and encourage the believers in other villages. I must continue teaching God's Word to the Man-ofar people. I might die at any time, and there is still so much more they need to know about the Lord.

"The believers here are growing well because they easily understand God's Word when our own language is read. We, who believe His Word from the time we were baptized, put aside the customs of our forefathers. We no longer follow them, for it is not traditions that will save us. As God's Word tells us, it is only through Jesus Christ that we will be saved.

"Now we pray to God to help us and bless us, those whom He chose as His children."

As soon as he could get about, although that was with great difficulty, he resumed his ministry at Man-ofar. Instead of taking twenty minutes to hike there, it took him over two hours stumbling and crawling along the rough trail.

Ammoya died in May 1985, two years after his stroke. We wish we could have been at his funeral. Udchus described it as "a believer's funeral." He said, "Everyone knew that the Lord was there."

ELEVEN
Cause for Rejoicing

Manila, here we come!

In June 1982 the time came to make a decision we had long dreaded. We didn't want to be separated from any of our children because of their education, but David had completed Year 8 at school, and there seemed no alternative but to send him to Faith Academy in Manila. He could board in one of the homes for missionaries' children there.

We had almost reached the inevitable but still unwanted decision to let him go away, when it suddenly occurred to us that we could go with him, and keep our family together after all. We couldn't be in Mallango, and there was really nothing to keep us in Bagabag. We just hoped that people from Mallango would be happy to stay on the bus the extra six hours to Manila instead of stopping at Bagabag.

We made the move, and our friends from Mallango didn't mind the opportunity to see Manila each time they came to work with us.

We continued working on the translation, though it wasn't ideal doing it away from the village and the interaction of people. However, we had good help. Udchus promised to see the work through to completion. He said he had committed his life to completing the New Testament.

As we completed each portion of the New Testament, we printed lots of copies and sent them back for the elders to use. That would give the translation a good test for comprehension and accuracy. Quite a pile of small books soon resulted. However, the elders found they were not adept at juggling too many publications under their arms, and they appealed to us, "Please, no more little books. It's getting hard to carry so many books. We want the whole New Testament, in one volume."

The believers grew both in number and in maturity. They stopped sacrificing when they believed in God, and after a while even unbelievers began to stop the practice. By 1986 sacrificing had virtually ceased because there was a scarcity of shamans available to serve as spirit mediums. Of the twelve shamans in the five villages with which we were the most familiar, eleven believed. The one remaining practitioner was too old to hike far from his village.

Even the spirits seemed to be giving ground to God. Udchus told us, "Before the Gospel made its impact on the Mallango people, no one would venture outside at night from fear of the spirits. Sometimes the spirits seemed to fill the village. Since many have believed, even unbelievers will go outside at night. Now only a few sacrifice. Once when a shaman was called to Mallango from a distant village, she was unable to contact any spirits and concluded that the spirits must have gone to a faraway place."

Each time Udchus and others came to work with us, they brought stories of changed lives. Some were on audiotape, taped during services in the villages. There were many testimonies and we listened to them with great joy.

Kodyam

Kodyam told of when he used to be a killer. "In our place," he said, "killers were honoured, so that's the reason people wanted to kill others. After we killed a person, we were tattooed on our arms and upper body so that everyone who saw us would recognise us as warriors. Since I had killed many people, I was considered a great warrior, so when I spoke in any gathering everyone listened to me.

"When the Word of God was brought to Mallango, some believed it and then they came to my village to tell the Good

196

News. Some accepted that what they were teaching was the truth and they believed in Jesus Christ. I was one of those, but I didn't tell anyone. After that I went every Sunday with many others to Mallango to listen to God's Word being read and explained. People probably wondered why I went as I gave no indication that I believed in Jesus Christ.

"Then there was a tribal war between my village and another. Some of the weaker believers turned from their faith and went to fight the enemy. However, some of the men, including those who stood firm in their faith, didn't go off to fight. Instead they guarded the edge of our village. That's what I did. One night as I sat there alone with plenty of time to think, I began to have doubts about what I had heard and believed and I wondered if this teaching was really true.

"One of the men sent to guard the border one night was also a believer. During the night he fell asleep. When he woke up next morning, he noticed footprints all around where he lay. Later that day he said to me, 'God protected me because I believe in Him.'

"I believed what he related to me and my doubts were removed. Then I decided to be baptised. When I told people about my decision, and they realised that I really did believe, many others also believed. In the past, I was one of the leaders in the village. Now I am one of the leaders in the church.

"One day I went to Udchus and I asked him, 'When will the New Testament be completed in one book? I want to have it all to read.' He answered, 'Just be patient, and use the portions that have already been printed, for it takes much time to complete a whole New Testament.' I kept on reading what had been translated already, so that my faith would not become weak."

Luki

Old Luki was a gentle giant of a man. He said: "I was one of the hardest to convince. Whatever was said about God, I didn't believe it. I would say, 'We have known God for a long time. There's no new God. As long as we don't do anything bad, like stealing, then that's enough.' I was a very proud man because I was a very industrious worker.

"Because I was well-off, when a poor person tried to talk to me about salvation I would say to him, 'Talk to yourself first. Even though you don't do anything bad, you're still poor!' What I meant was, 'Why do you teach me? I know what I'm doing, and I know how to become rich. But your words are useless; you teach, and you have nothing.'

"Then after a while, one of the believers who was also well-off came and told me about the Good News. I had nothing to say then. Instead, I listened to God's Word, and I realised I was not good and that I had a bad standing in God's presence.

"Because of hearing God's Word I repented of my sins and I believed in Jesus, and trusted Him for my forgiveness. Now I do everything that a believer should do. My whole attitude has changed. I no longer have pride in myself. Now I am encouraging the other believers in my village."

Chawakan

Chawakan said: "I was known as a peacemaker in my village. I am an old man, and others say that I'm very wise. Although I knew God existed, I would have nothing to do with Him. I used to insult the believers, challenging them about whether they really understood God's Word. They often tried to convince me to come to a service to hear what was said, but I wouldn't go.

"One Sunday while the church service was on, I was in my house. Around mid-morning, I fainted. As I lay unconscious on the floor, I heard a voice. It said, 'You, Chawakan, you are insulting My words! You are insulting Me! Are you trying to destroy the faith of those who worship Me? Are you trying to prevent people from worshipping Me? Even your own family?'

"In my unconscious state I thought I was about to die. I said to the One speaking to me, 'God, I will no longer insult those who worship you. I will also worship You. Whatever You say, I will do. Whatever You want me to do, I will do. I will obey You from this time on.'

"Then I recovered and went outside. A child was passing by my house, and I again heard the voice. This time it said to me, 'Follow that child. He will lead you to My house. I will show you what I want you to do, and you must obey. You are to observe those who teach my Word, and you will help them.'

"From that time on I knew God was real, and I believed in Him and worshipped Him."

Fanut

Fanut's testimony was also encouraging. "My wife Chammiyog and I used to fight all the time," he said. "We hated each other, and we hated everyone else. Everyone else hated us, too, because we always wanted to quarrel with them.

"When we accepted Jesus Christ, we stopped quarrelling. People could hardly believe it! So many were amazed that our tongues were now controlled and we treated our children well. When they observed us closely and saw how much we had changed, some said, 'Yes, it's true! Their minds have truly been changed. They are following God's way.'

"Some who didn't believe in God scoffed, saying, 'Is it only now that their God came, so that it's only now that they stop fighting?' Those who understood what had happened to us knew the truth. We had really believed in God, and that's why we had begun living the way God wants people to."

Magsaysay

When 30-year-old Magsaysay heard God's Word proclaimed, he was "happy to believe." Udchus said, "After Magsaysay believed, he did all the things a believer should do." He was enthusiastic about his new Christian life. Later, when distressing times fell on his village, some of the

Cause for Rejoicing

believers turned away from the Lord. When his father-in-law was shot dead by someone, Magsaysay also rejected his faith.

A few days later, he contracted a virus that left him almost blind. For help he turned to the shaman, who told him what he must do to appease the spirits before they would restore his sight. He obeyed. First he offered a hen, but that wasn't enough for the spirits. Over the next few days he killed a dog and a pig, but the spirits required more. They wanted his most valuable animal. "Kill a water buffalo!" they demanded.

Magsaysay obeyed and killed his water buffalo, but he still couldn't see. Now, with no more animals and no hope, he wondered what was to become of him. In his despair, he remembered the Word of the God in which he had recently believed.

The following Sunday he joined the believers from his village going to the service in Mallango. As he was led falteringly along the once-familiar trail that meandered around the edges of rice terraces, he sensed that a message of hope awaited him at the end of his journey.

The theme of that morning's Bible study was the persecution and suffering that Christians can expect. Sitting there in his darkened world, Magsaysay saw his life in a new light, and he repented. At the end of the service he stood up and confessed that he had failed God, and that he wanted to turn back to Him. He asked the elders to pray for him. The elders encircled him, placed their hands on his head and prayed for his healing, just as they had learned through their study of the Scriptures.

The following Sunday Magsaysay needed no guide. He could see the trail to Mallango as clearly as his rejoicing companions. That day, he witnessed publicly to his faith by being baptised.

The last audiotape we received from the believers included the prayers of two men, Fanut and Tasiyu. Fanut prayed, "The words of Jesus Christ are the only way, and Your words, our Father God, are the only food. I thank You, God, that Bruce and Judith came to make known the Word of God to us in Kalinga. Give wisdom to those members of SIL who are working for Your Word, and give Bruce and Judith joy also through Your Word that they sowed here in Kalinga. Give them wisdom too, and encourage them to come and visit their brothers and sisters here so we can see each other, so that our faith will be strengthened. And we also thank You, God, for not permitting what was to happen when Bruce came to Filung."

Then he had a message for us: "We pray for you. Pray also for us, so that our faith will grow and not be destroyed. We have experienced much persecution this year, but we have not given up. Instead, it has strengthened our faith."

Tasiyu prayed, "Our God, we are happy with Your Word which Bruce and Judith brought to our place. We thank You, God, for sending Your Son Jesus Christ here to Kalinga."

We left for Australia in December 1984. The New Testament was almost ready for publication, but we felt it needed further testing before sending it to press. In May 1987, the first copies of the Southern Kalinga New Testament found their way into the hands of grateful readers. We would love to have been there to see that.

The encouragement continues

In March 1986, Masa-aw from Balangao and Ilat from Ifugao made a much-appreciated journey of encouragement to Mallango. We were not in the Philippines at that time, but Jo Shetler, who worked in Balangao, wrote us a short but extremely welcome report about their trip, beginning with the words, "At last they did it! They went to

Cause for Rejoicing

Mallango!" She added, "I had pleaded with them for a long time to go, but their excuses for not going were always good. Now they have gone, and I'm not sure who is happier— them or me! They found it both encouraging and exciting."

As the two boarded the bus in Bontoc for the 56 km trip north, some people warned them, "Tinglayan people butcher people on buses!" Ilat thought about that for a moment, and then decided he wouldn't let that warning stop him from going.

It was dark when they alighted from the bus, thankful for an uneventful trip. Since they didn't know the area, they became disorientated, but a man from Mallango came along and guided them to the home of Palongpong.

Dozens of people converged on the house, wanting to talk to them even before they ate. They were finally allowed to eat before heading to the church so that more could meet with them. Mallango believers began sharing their burdens with their visitors, continuing until midnight, and then some followed them back to Palongpong's home where they talked until 2 a.m.

After breakfast, over 70 adults went to the church again for a Bible study instead of to their fields. It continued through the day and into the night, again until 2 a.m. After a brief sleep Masa-aw and Ilat were invited to Arngikan, the next village south, where they shared the Gospel until noon. Then they hiked further south to Sumachor for a brief study before going on to Filung, the village where the two men had tried to kill me six years before.

Over 80 gathered. Masa-aw and Ilat planned to spend that afternoon and evening at Filung, then return to Mallango next morning, being Sunday, for the service—but the Filung people wouldn't let them leave. They begged their visitors to stay longer, and sent a message to Mallango telling them that if they wanted to hear the visitors speak on Sunday, the Mallango people would have to come to Filung. Many did. Then on the

Cause for Rejoicing

Sunday afternoon, the men were "allowed" to go to Mallango, and they returned to their home villages the following morning.

Epilogue

Dreams can come true!

In 1993 we visited Mallango again. The main reason for my Philippines trip was to represent Wycliffe Australia at the Bontoc New Testament Dedication. However, with Mallango only 56 km from Bontoc, our children paid Judith's fare so she could go with me. What a blessing.

What had seemed an "impossible dream" came true when we flew into Mallango. It was only a 22-hour visit—but we're grateful to the Lord for it.

In the evening we enjoyed a three-hour impromptu program by the believers. The testimonies in word and song about God, His Word, their faith and their tributes to us for helping to provide the Word of God for them, were beautiful to hear.

One said, "We thank God for sending Bruce and Judith to Mallango. If they had not come to translate the Word of God into our language, we would not know about Jesus Christ. Don't think that it was easy for them. When I stayed with them, I saw their weariness, their hardships, their many tears, the many times they prayed. They worked day and night to get the Word of God translated for us so that we would have the opportunity to believe in God. That was their great desire, so we thank God for them. Even though we are only a small village, God blessed us by sending them here, and we can see the fruits of their work for many have believed in Him through reading the Word of God. How privileged we are that God sent this family to share His love with us."

Although we didn't look for such comments, we needed to hear them! At last we were able to see our work's end—even

Epilogue

though, praise God, it has *not* ended and will *never* end. Such is the impact of the Kalinga people now having the Scriptures.

One young fellow said, "How great is God's love that He allowed Bruce and Judith to come and visit us. We can see how much they love us. We see by their tears how much they have missed us—and we have also missed them."

After an absence of 13 years, there were lots of things we wanted to do and people we wanted to talk to, but where do you start when it's been 13 years and you're only there for one day? We believe our visit encouraged many of the believers. We were definitely encouraged.

The church continues to grow and has spread to most of the other villages in the language group. At present there are more than 1,000 believers.

The testimonies of our children add to our assurance that it was worth persevering in the hard times. Seeing the impact of the Bible translated into the Kalinga language allowed our young children to clearly see what the Word of God could do—instilling in them a love for God's Word.

We're all grateful to God for taking us to the Kalinga people—not only for the special Kalinga coffee we loved—but also for the privilege of being part of God's ongoing ministry in people's lives as a result of the translated Word of God.

Afterword

by the Director of Wycliffe Australia

I first met Bruce and Judith Grayden when they were studying at the SIL school in Brisbane in 1971. I didn't know at the time what a significant introduction that would be. After all, I was only eleven and was at the school only because my father was the principal. However, I met up with the Graydens again in 1991. This time Bruce was my "boss," as I had taken up an assignment in Wycliffe Australia's Media Department that he was leading.

The Kalinga story, and the Grayden family's involvement in it, is one that needs to be told. Therefore, I am pleased to see that Bruce's dream of writing this book is now a reality. This story needs to be read and contemplated, because it is a story of hope, of perseverance, of doing whatever it takes to get the Word of God into the hands of a people group. It is also a story of watching God work through His Word in a people group.

We are standing at an important crossroad in history. The Bible translation effort has been going on for 2,300 years! Yet 3,000 of the world's 6,800 languages still do not have one word of Scripture. That is incredible when you consider all the modern technology, the ease of transport, a global church emerging. Yet, at the current rate of activity, it will take another 150 years to complete the task of Bible translation. That is unacceptable. To address this, Wycliffe and SIL International (Wycliffe's sister organization) embraced the vision that by the year 2025 a Bible translation project will be in progress for every people group that needs it. We call this

Afterword

Vision 2025. It is dependent upon people of all nations becoming more involved than ever before in the Bible translation and literacy task.

I trust you were inspired by the story contained in the pages of this book, but more importantly, that you are challenged to deepen your walk with God and that you will respond to the Lord Jesus' challenge to address the fact that His workers are few.

Kirk Franklin
Executive Director
Wycliffe Bible Translators Australia